IN HIS SHELTER

ELLAMAE ELDER

In loving memory of

Gene,

the only man I ever loved.

ACKNOWLEDGEMENTS

When I was nineteen, God brought my future husband into my life. I was in college, waiting for a ride to church. When my friend pulled up, a handsome man was riding with him. The man jumped out, gave me his seat, and crawled in the back. As we headed off, he called out, "I'm Eugene Elder, and I was wondering who that pretty lady is in the front seat." That day began our love story and eventual life journey as partners in ministry. In our later years, when our children were adults, we went to South Africa as missionaries. We were married sixty-three years. Gene was the love of my life. I will always be grateful for Gene's abiding love and devotion and that the Lord brought us together.

I'm grateful to our children—David, Joy, and Tim. They gave us their blessing to go overseas as missionaries. They were forced to say goodbye to us many times so we could be obedient to God's call on our lives. I am very proud of them and their families. During our time in South Africa, they blessed us with seven grandchildren.

I owe a debt of gratitude to my mother and daddy, Haywood and Inez Thompson, who reared me with biblical values and principles. As a nine-year-old, Mother answered my questions about how to become a Christian. It was in my home church that I became a Christian and first felt God's call to missions.

Pastors of my church faithfully preached the gospel. They encouraged and inspired me in my Christian-walk, especially Pastor Merton Griffin.

I'm grateful for my Sunday school teachers and Training Union leaders (now Discipleship Training). My mother was my Girls Auxiliary leader, later known as Girls in Actions or GAs. Mrs. Kathleen Morgan was my Acteens leader. These women devoted untold time and energy.

I'm grateful for my Vacation Bible School (VBS) teachers and principals. The VBS principals always told mission stories. When I was ten years of age, one principal, Willie Dee Till, told a particularly interesting mission story. Afterwards, I felt God calling me to a life of missions.

I'm grateful for Shocco Springs camp in Alabama where God confirmed my call to foreign missions (now referred to as international missions).

I'm grateful for the churches who nurtured me spiritually, especially Ebenezer East Baptist Church, Greenville, Alabama and First Baptist Church, Aztec, New Mexico.

I'm thankful for the many friendships God provided during our time in South Africa. I found new friends in my Bible, sewing, and literacy classes. I worked with ladies in the Baptist Women's Department (BWD) and other regional departments. During my last year in the country, I had the honor and privilege to serve as president of the South Africa Baptist Women's Department (SABWD).

Further, Gene and I made lasting connections through the many marriage enrichment seminars we conducted. We also worked with pastors and lay leaders in the Continuing Witnessing Program that provided instruction on sharing the gospel message. We rejoiced together when many people came to Jesus through this program.

Always a tireless servant, Gene was a pastor for family camps and led workshops for deacons and Sunday school leaders. During our last three years in South Africa, he directed Theological Education by Extension at the Cape Town Baptist College (now Cape Town Baptist Seminary). Our hearts swelled with gratitude when we remembered all of these dear souls.

I'm grateful for our missionary colleagues who were like family to us. We shared dinners, birthdays, camps, mission meetings, and prayer. I was challenged by their commitment to missions and their love for God.

And finally, I'm immensely thankful God made me His born-again child and called me to be a missionary. Gene and I were ordinary people, but God used us in extraordinary ways to bring honor and glory to His name. He is the reason I wrote this book.

TABLE OF CONTENTS

Acknowledgements vii

Chapter One: Mission Call 1

Chapter Two: A New Beginning 11

Chapter Three: Barachel 18

Chapter Four: Sewing Stitches in Ciskei 24

Chapter Five: Chalumna 31

Chapter Six: Easter Weekend 39

Chapter Seven: Out of Ruins 47

Chapter Eight: A Christmas Memory 53

Chapter Nine: Nelson Mandela 57

Chapter Ten: Coup in the Ciskei 61

Chapter Eleven: Jesus Film 66

Chapter Twelve: Burned Shacks 69

Chapter Thirteen: Illness in the Manse 90

Chapter Fourteen: Reaping in the Harvest 102

Chapter Fifteen: A Letter to My Children 109

Chapter Sixteen: Stateside Assignment 113

Chapter Seventeen: Mother's Day 1993 119

Chapter Eighteen: Mission Meeting 1994 128

Chapter Nineteen: Peace and Freedom at Last..........................132

Chapter Twenty: A Light in the Darkness 136

Chapter Twenty-One: The Youth at Dongwe 144

Chapter Twenty-Two: Ministry at Bubele 149

Chapter Twenty-Three: An Uninvited Visitor.........................156

Chapter Twenty-Four: A Treasured Friendship in Cape Town.. 160

Chapter Twenty-Five: Ladies Seminar.......................................164

Chapter Twenty-Six: Two Weeks of Wonder 170

Chapter Twenty-Seven: Going Home 177

Epilogue 186

CHAPTER ONE

MISSION CALL

*He who dwells in the shelter of the Most High
will rest in the shadow of the Almighty.
Psalm 91:1*

"The light has gone out of your eyes."

It was Sunday evening when my thoughts rolled off my tongue. My husband Gene, a pastor of our church for the last twelve years, had led a deacons' training session for several weeks.

"You're right," Gene said.

"What's bothering you?"

"The deacons seemed resistant to trying new programs. I think they've followed me as far as they're going to." Hesitating, he added, "I love the church, but I need a change. I still have a lot of drive and energy."

We had been in ministry for twenty-six years. In 1958, Gene had taught at a private Christian school so I could get my teaching credentials. In 1960, while he studied for his pastoral degree at New Orleans Baptist Theological Seminary, I taught school in St. Bernard parish. Following seminary, Gene served at his first pastorate in Pheba, Mississippi. Afterwards, we became missionaries of the Home Mission Board (now North American Mission Board) to Native Americans in New Mexico. Three subsequent pastorates had followed.

I thought to myself, *does "a change" mean leaving our house?* Sadness came over me as I looked around our home. Nine years earlier, we'd built it from the ground up. I kept telling myself that I mustn't fall in love with my home because God might move us to another place.

But inwardly, I had hoped we could retire in New Mexico. I loved the state, nicknamed the "Land of Enchantment," with its deserts, mountains, and mesas. I had reveled in windswept prairies and brilliant sunsets. In our community, I had parented, taught, and made treasured friends. My son David met his wife Pam at our church. They married, built a house nearby, and blessed us with our first precious grandchild, named after her grandfather. Jeannie was only nineteen months old. She knew the way to our house. I was quite comfortable in "my nest."

My thoughts turned to my other children. Joy, a lab technician in Galveston, Texas, was married to Mark, a medical student. Tim, our youngest son, attended Hardin-Simmons University in Abilene, Texas. How would they feel about us leaving?

The following week, Gene talked with James Tidenberg, a pastor friend who had been a missionary in Tanzania, Africa. He told James of our mission interest and need for a change. That day Gene came home excited. Hearing James's mission experiences revived our interest in international missions. When Gene and I met, we were mission volunteers. Later, as we took mission teams from our Aztec church to Korea, Brazil, and Mexico, we continued to wonder if mission work might be in our future. But God had not opened this door before. Now, for the first time in our marriage, we were seriously considering full-time missionary service overseas.

The next day Gene contacted the International Mission Board in Richmond, Virginia, for application papers. We filled them out promptly. Because of our age, we had to pass a preliminary screening that mainly dealt with health and mental issues.

Again, I became unsettled with gnawing thoughts. Where would we go? What continent? What country? What kind of house would we have? And what about our son's college expenses?

Mercifully, the Lord spoke to my anxious heart during my quiet time one day. "You will go out in joy and be led forth in peace…" (Isaiah 55:12). How much I would need those words in months to come.

After the Thanksgiving holidays, we called Joy and told her of our application to the mission board. "Is this your midlife crisis?" I could hear humor in her voice.

When Tim came home for Christmas vacation, I gave him the news. "Tell Dad to go for it," he said, smiling. "But I'd like both of you to return for my college graduation and for Dad to perform my wedding ceremony." He was also fine spending holidays at David's house.

When we shared the news with David and Pam, David responded, "I'm not surprised since you and Dad have always been involved in missions."

In the midst of my misgivings, I still felt excited when I thought about a change in ministry and of moving to another country. In our previous churches and missions, I had enjoyed socializing with people of other cultures even though a language barrier hindered communication. It pleased me that our children appeared happy for us. Yet I knew they would have different feelings once this idea became a reality.

When John Riddell, a candidate consultant, came to Albuquerque, New Mexico, we met with him for an interview. He helped guide us to a mission assignment in South Africa where Gene would fill a general evangelist position.

Going to South Africa thrilled me because we could speak English. Yet I had reservations about the country and wondered about safety. Shootings, bombings, and boycotts plastered the newspapers. I saw horrific scenes of Black-on-

Black violence on television. A particularly brutal form of torture called "necklacing" involved lighting a gasoline-soaked tire that had been placed around a person's neck. The fire burned until the person died.

We studied the job assignments John had sent us about three places in South Africa—East London, Port Elisabeth, and Cape Town. Because we wanted to be absolutely certain about which city, Gene and I prayed alone about this decision. The Director of Missions in East London had requested a missionary five years earlier. We read his most recent letter to our mission board asking when the position would be filled. That letter influenced our decision. East London also matched the requests we had asked of the Lord. It had a temperate climate, a low altitude, and a challenging ministry. We agreed East London was to be our new home and place of service.

Not only was I concerned about leaving our children, especially Tim, but also about leaving my mother who suffered from Alzheimer's. She had nurtured my interest in missions and was not able to share in my joy of missionary service. She lived with my brother's family. When we prepared to leave, I felt I was abandoning her as well as my brother Percy and his wife Ada Sue. I was afraid she wouldn't survive our first term.

Further, I didn't want to leave my close friend Joan[1] who had multiple sclerosis. A couple of months after we moved to Aztec, Joan came to visit me. She told me how she'd had

---

[1] Name has been changed.

trouble walking and was afraid of what her diagnosis might be. When she went into the hospital for tests, she told her doctor she thought she had multiple sclerosis. Her self-diagnosis was correct. I had visited her often and watched her decline. In a matter of a year, she was confined to a wheelchair and struggled to eat with her left hand since she was right-handed. She also used a chain to transfer herself from the bed or sofa into her wheelchair.

As the weeks progressed, I continued to mull over our decision. Was it strange that we would become international missionaries at this point in life? And yet it wasn't strange. I had felt God's call during a mission story when I was only ten years old at Vacation Bible School.

But how would we minister to the Black community? I had grown up in Alabama and attended segregated schools. With my background, I could understand the racial issues surrounding apartheid, and living in New Mexico had helped diminish racial prejudice. But still, we had no direct experience.

Further, I worried about our ages. "How can we go to the mission field now?" I asked Gene. "We have passed the age limit for appointment by the mission board."

Gene had an answer ready and told me about the new program for applicants with our education and experience who had passed the age cut off. It was called the associate career program. With that assurance, we moved forward.

Soon the day came to notify our church, since we had listed a few church members as references. Officials at the mission board had warned us how the congregation might react. Our announcement might be viewed as an official departure. But if we weren't appointed, would our ministry at the church be over? To move into the unknown was bold and scary.

Waiting for the mission board's approval felt like drifting out to sea on an iceberg. I was concerned about the future. The church was doing well in discipleship and community outreach, but we sensed they were ready for new leadership and new ideas.

After several weeks, John Riddell called. "You've been approved. The trustees have voted yes to your going to South Africa."

From the time we sent in our applications to the final approval was nine months. Most applications took eighteen months. This accelerated approval confirmed our calling, both to the church and to us. Gene was relieved, excited, and elated. I was mostly relieved that we had been approved.

Days flew by as I became more aware of what I would miss when I left the country. When I listened to Gene give the children's sermons each Sunday, I watched the children's faces closely. At Easter, I attended my last sunrise service in the Kiva of the Anasazi Indians at Aztec Ruins. I would never again see that big cross cast its shadow on the people assembled there.

Soon, our home resembled a tornado zone. We stored items in our garage and packed other items in a crate that would be shipped overseas. On the last day, when our house went up for rent, we left to visit friends and relatives before going to orientation at the Missionary Learning Center, now International Learning Center (ILC), in Rockville, Virginia.

On the autumn day we arrived at ILC, we saw red-leafed oaks along the roadways. We would live in an apartment building with three other families and share a common great room. No televisions or radios were allowed. Over the next seven weeks, we completed a forty-hour course outside of the daily classes that met from 8:30 a.m. to 4:00 p.m. with a break for lunch.

On Sundays, we attended churches of other faiths, and at night, we had worship services at ILC. We visited a Jewish temple for a Bar Mitzvah. One cold Sunday, we ventured a bus ride to Washington D.C. to visit a Hindu temple, a Muslim mosque, and the National Cathedral. While there, we saw homeless people. I couldn't help but blurt out to Gene, "Of all places, we shouldn't have homeless people here. Can't we as a nation take care of them?"

Gene reminded me that these activities were a microcosm of the community and of the church and were designed to prepare us for missionary service. Back home in New Mexico, our work with Hispanics and Native Americans had also prepared us.

Gene and I enjoyed our experience at ILC and learned a great deal. We were also grateful for the many new friends we made. All too soon, our intensive training ended, and we headed back to Aztec.

We celebrated Christmas at David's house. Tim came from college and Joy and her husband arrived from Galveston. Our family helped us pack our suitcases and trunks and weigh each item to ensure we remained within the allotted weight allowance. We also filled out change-of-address cards. Then it was time for our departure.

On a cold morning eight days later, David drove us to the airport in Durango, Colorado, while the rest of the family drove behind us. We left at 4:00 a.m. and found the roads to be snow packed most of the way. That morning when Pam awakened Jeannie, she said, "Us go back to sleep."

At the airport, Gene checked our luggage to Johannesburg, South Africa, and we snuggled together for our final moments before boarding. When the time came to say goodbye, Joy, who was expecting a baby, was sick and began to cry. I thought of the many times I had comforted her as a little girl, and now I was the cause of her crying.

I stared at David, who held Jeannie in his arms. He looked so sad. Tim seemed as crestfallen as his brother. I hugged them both, then walked through the double doors to the plane.

I looked back for one final glimpse of my family, but I couldn't see them through the dark glass. Snow fell as we walked on the concourse. I listened to the small airplane's drone and wondered how it could possibly make it to Denver.

Because of my tears, I could barely see the gray clouds engulfing the plane as we climbed skyward on that December day in 1987. The plane was so small that Gene and I were not able to sit together. When I looked over at him, he was crying too.

We began our mission assignment in tears, but they would not be the only tears we would shed over the next fourteen years. Our lives would radically change and nothing could have prepared me for Africa and the days that followed.

Chapter Two

A NEW BEGINNING

I will say of the Lord He is my refuge and my fortress,
my God, in whom I trust.
Psalm 91:2

January 1, 1988

"We can see the mainland now!" Gene said. "Come and see the view on the other side of the plane." I followed him down the aisle to where Haskell and Elaine Wilson sat. In April of 1987, we met them at the candidates' conference. Later in August, we had each received our missionary appointment at the Glorieta Conference Center in Glorieta, New Mexico.

I peered out their window. "It's so green!"

Soon, the KLM plane began its descent toward the runway to Jan Smuts International Airport (now Johannesburg O.R. Tambo International Airport). After we passed through the passport control station, we retrieved our luggage and met

Don Moore and Cliff Staton from the Baptist International Mission Services (BIMS).

For two weeks, we made arrangements and then headed to East London, a city on the southeast coast of South Africa. Driving a compact car and pulling a trailer on "the wrong side of the road" proved challenging. As we drove along, we enjoyed the green and gorgeous countryside and the lovely yards in the small towns. After we had traveled several hours, we came to the Karoo desert that looked like the desert of New Mexico. Thankfully, we didn't have much traffic as we were eager to see our new home. As we neared, I tried to envision East London. Would it be flat or hilly? And the coastline, would it look like Florida, California, or Massachusetts?

Soon we arrived and were amazed by East London's beauty. It stretched up hilly terrain and overlooked the Indian Ocean. Later, wherever we would roam in the city, we could see the sparkling emerald sea and the alabaster beaches that looked like the Florida coast. They were breathtaking.

Our house awaited us in Beacon Bay, a hilltop suburb of East London. While driving there, we passed a modern mall with a quaint restaurant and fabric shop. Past these, we noted a large grocery store and other businesses. They, too, looked modern. I also watched a woman exit the grocery store with a baby on her back and groceries in hand. She hustled to a bus stop while workers lounged nearby, talking and laughing under sprawling palm trees. Near the tops of the trees, long and curvy leaf-covered limbs displayed their splendor.

We were so excited to find our home on our new street, Mayflower Terrace. When we pulled into our new driveway, I recalled the Pilgrims who sailed for months on the Mayflower ship. Their heroism would help build a nation in America. I thought of their courage and perseverance as they built houses, a church, and grew food in a strange land. Would I display fortitude and bravery in my new venture as they had? Would I help build God's kingdom in South African hearts, plant churches in the country's lush soil, and sow the sweet seeds of Jesus' Word in this city?

Just as the flowers of East London seemed different from the flora of New Mexico, the language of "nationals" (South African natives) seemed very different. The next morning, I heard the cheerful sounds of a language I didn't understand. And perhaps like Joseph in Egypt, the reality of living in a new city and country stirred my imagination. Growing up in the southern United States, I knew the familiar accent of African Americans, but here the people spoke with strange clicks.

Even the nature of the workforce seemed different. Each day, maids and gardeners commuted by buses from the townships for work in the White suburb. Sometimes a maid lived in a small apartment at the rear of the residence where she worked, but the majority had to travel long distances.

Besides the Black workforce, I became aware of the tentacles of apartheid that entangled every stratum of South African society. The government had designated people into four racial classes—Whites, Colored (mixed race), Asians, and Blacks. Living under apartheid etched fear into the faces of many people.

In 1984, the government declared a state of emergency, effectively banning political organizations from meetings. As unrest continued, the ensuing years brought more "crackdowns" and restrictions. The government began targeting and detaining thousands of people for ninety days or longer without their family's knowledge. They restricted political funerals and imposed curfews. In Black communities, they prohibited national and international media coverage of increasing police oppression. South Africa had evolved into a totalitarian state under White minority rule. I wondered how God could possibly use me—a White woman—in this heated political climate.

Many countries had initiated economic sanctions against South Africa. By January 1987, ninety-six American companies had halted business. No longer did corporate Americans and their families live in the country. The United States also prohibited South African Airways access to any US domestic airports, and no American airlines flew to South Africa. Ripped apart by racial and political turmoil, South Africa had become isolated from the world.

Apartheid affected my daily life, too. As newcomers, Black maids and gardeners watched our house, hoping to find work. One day, the doorbell rang. At the door, a Black lady greeted me, "Good morning, madam."

"Good morning."

"I am looking for a job as a maid."

"Oh, I'm sorry. At present, I don't think I need one yet. I hope you find work."

The woman hung her head wearily, turned, and ambled down the steps toward the bus stop. This scene would repeat itself numerous times in the months and years ahead. Men would come, seeking work as a gardener. Others would come for food, clothes, or money.

Apart from daily challenges, I experienced loneliness and culture shock. For reassurance, I recalled what I had learned at the ILC. Our survival in another country depended upon our relationships with its people. We also learned that we needed to forget our past experiences and move forward in our present reality. God confirmed these truths during my quiet time one morning when I read, "Forget the former things: do not dwell on the past. See, I am doing a new thing! Now it springs up: do you not perceive it? I am making a way in the desert and streams in the wasteland." (Isaiah 43:18-19). At the time, I was living the "new thing" and didn't realize it.

Part of God's way "in the desert" involved learning new skills. On March 6, 1988, I wrote the following in a letter to friends:

These six weeks I have been in Beacon Bay, a suburb of East London, I have learned how to drive on the left side of the road with a stick shift, cook in metric, shop in metric with a new currency, adapt to a different system of electricity, operate an electric typewriter and a new detailed radio and cassette player, and the most important of all, to stay alone in another country while my husband traveled to Zimbabwe.

I worked at trying to "forget the former things," but each morning, I nearly jumped when I heard the postal motorcycle at mail time. One day, a letter came from Tim. At the bottom of the page, a stick figure sat at a desk. From a window next to the desk, a conversation balloon emerged. It said, "Hi! Just remember this is where I live." Next to this, Tim had drawn four bare trees. I knew he must feel lonely and abandoned in his dorm. Guilt struck me. I prayed earnestly for him.

My loneliness persisted. One autumn day in May, Gene and I strolled barefoot along Bonza Bay beach with the wind at our backs. We listened as waves splashed against the rocks and dashed to shore. A flock of seagulls ran in front of us. One hopped along, trying to keep up with the others. We soon discovered that it had a missing leg. I could feel God speaking in that moment: *I know you must feel like the seagull does without the former things. You will make it. You have not moved away from my presence, my power, or my protection. You will readjust to your life here and overcome like this seagull.*

If I were to overcome those feelings, I knew I needed to seek the Lord in prayer. I recalled Psalm 91:11—that angels watched over us. This verse and the rest of Psalm 91 inspired and encouraged me and became my favorite scripture during my South African years. Before dawn each day, I went to my guest room for a quiet time of prayer and Bible meditation. I felt like the Psalmist David when he prayed, "I long to dwell in Your tent forever and take refuge in the shelter of Your wings." (Psalm 61:4).

Gracious people and immense beauty embraced me, but only the Lord could ease my loneliness. I found safety and security in the shelter of the Almighty.

CHAPTER THREE

BARACHEL

*I tell you the truth, unless an ear of wheat falls to
the ground and dies, it remains only a single seed.*
John 12:24

At 4:30 a.m. on May 22, I traveled with eight ladies to a camp near Johannesburg. The nine of us squeezed into an eight-passenger van for a six-hundred-mile trip. I had debated whether or not to go since they were leaving quite early, and I felt like "the odd man out." But wasn't I here to minister to "the nationals," these women of South Africa? The Lord had already made that clear.

At 5:30 p.m., we arrived at Barachel. It was time for dinner, but first we stopped by our assigned rooms. I'm not sure I concealed my surprise when I saw the three-tiered bunk beds in a small room. Near these beds, each woman had a tiny cubbyhole to store her belongings. But where were the bathrooms? I soon learned—in another building.

Happily, a few minutes later, Jackie Shaw, a colleague of our mission, came into the room. I was relieved and delighted to see her familiar face and gave her a hug. Jackie chose the bottom bed, and I volunteered to climb to the top bed, even without a ladder. No one occupied the middle bed.

We ate dinner in the covered courtyard, and each woman brought her own dishes, cutlery, and dish towel. After the meal, I followed the other ladies to clean my dishes in the soapy bleached water of the community washtub.

As we entered the room for the evening session, a lady held a box of pictures. Stressing the importance of partnering in prayer, she asked each woman to select half of a picture. She then instructed us to look for the person with the matching half. Immediately, I found my prayer partner, Shirley.

I found it interesting that of the 130 women in attendance, many were knitting. The women in charge didn't seem to mind. They opened the session with a welcome followed by singing, prayer, and a Bible devotion.

The next day at lunch, I ate with Shirley. We had an outdoor table near the lush green branches of a tree. This felt more like my memories of "camp."

A beautiful blonde, Shirley was tall, trim, and vivacious, and I was impressed and awed by her confident nature. She was from Kimberley, home of the "Big Hole," an open pit and underground South African diamond mine.

I learned that Shirley was a pastor's wife and taught school at Kimberley. She had two children and her husband's name was Bruce.

I shared with Shirley that I had taught elementary school for years, had three children, and had been a pastor's wife. Shirley and I thought the Lord had matched us well even though we came from different countries.

When I mentioned to Shirley how I missed my little granddaughter, her empathy touched me. I couldn't help but open my heart to her. I mentioned my lack of understanding the accent of "South African English" and how embarrassed I felt when asking people to repeat themselves…up to three times! When I spoke, people knew straightaway that I wasn't a South African. And I even goofed in table manners. I noticed Shirley ate with a fork in her left hand and a knife in her right. I ended by saying, "I'm always making mistakes. I feel out of place here."

Shirley clasped my hand and said, "Let's pray right now about this matter." As a cool autumn breeze rustled the leaves, my new prayer partner prayed fervently for me to adjust and adapt to South Africa.

As we were praying, a woman walked up to our table. After finishing, Shirley introduced the woman to me. Carol, Shirley's sister, was also a pastor's wife with three children. I found Carol's joyful spirit much like Shirley's, and they were both easy to talk to. What a blessing to have these new friends!

In the afternoon session, the East London ladies wanted to include me in the program. Rather than give the words I had prepared, I shared how I felt like "the new kid in town." I also told them my thirtieth wedding anniversary was the next day, and for the first time in our married life, I would be apart from Gene.

Doubt gnawed at me when I sat down. *Why in the world did I talk about my feelings?* Was it rude to express myself so openly? Surely, the women would reject me for my self-centeredness.

After the meeting ended, I met Jackie back in our room. She had her electric tea kettle and a long extension cord. In one smooth move, she placed the kettle on the floor and plugged the cord in next door.

"Jackie, you sure know how to 'camp' in South Africa."

She smiled, while handing me a cup of tea, and replied sweetly, "I've lived in Africa thirty years, and I always take my tea kettle and paraphernalia to serve coffee or tea." What a wonderful ministry—traveling hospitality. During several sessions, Jackie would sit quietly, stitching a needlepoint design of Table Mountain in Cape Town. She would later mentor me during her remaining time in South Africa.

What I could not have imagined when I "bared my soul" during the afternoon session was the loving and caring ways the ladies would respond to my "transparency." When we lined up to fill our plates at dinner, many of them chatted with me. My honesty had opened the door to more friendships. Before the week was over, I had met most of the women. I chuckled at how God had changed my attitude. Many of my new friends invited me to visit them!

On Wednesday evening, we were encouraged to turn in prayer requests for a prayer time during the Thursday morning session. We prayed as a large group. One request was for a three-year-old girl with leukemia. Immediately, an Indian pastor's wife stood to pray. Sadly, she had lost her three-year-old daughter to the same disease. To see this demonstration of God's power touched me deeply.

The session continued in amazing ways. Some women shared their testimonies. Others taught training sessions. I particularly enjoyed a Bible study on faith, led by the President of the Baptist Women of South Africa. And we sang. It was a beautiful sound.

As the week concluded, I couldn't help but compare what I had seen at the women's camp to what I had read in books about South Africa and apartheid. It was radically different. Ladies of all four classes of people dined, slept, and met together. In that setting, they loved each other, and they worshiped together with one faith and in one Lord. A spirit of unity sweetened the air. The week became a highlight of the year as I moved toward loving and accepting the people and the mission God had called me to fill.

The sky was overcast when we left on Saturday, and the road out of Roodeport looked different somehow. Free of my anxiety, I could appreciate the bright autumn colors—orange, gold, and brown.

By the time we reached the Karoo desert, the sun had begun its descent. Vibrant colors illuminated the sky in a way that only God could design.

The miles melted away. Feeling a peace I had not known before, I worked on crocheting an afghan for my daughter Joy's soon-to-be-born baby. As the afghan grew, I knew my love for South Africa and her people would also grow. This thought filled my heart as I admired the silvery gold sunset.

Chapter Four

SEWING STITCHES IN CISKEI

Peter went with them, and when he arrived he was taken upstairs to the room. All the widows stood around him, crying and showing him the robes and other clothing that Dorcas had made while she was still with them.
Acts 9:39

"*Where do I begin?*" That thought consumed me. As I daily observed the throng of needy people, my heart went out to them. The unemployment rate among the Blacks stood at seventy percent. If I could teach the women a skill, they could help provide for their families. Lionel Grunewald, a co-worker, reported that the Border Baptist Association of churches had started a sewing machine ministry. They needed help to distribute the machines as well as someone to teach sewing classes. I loved to sew, and I had made many garments for my children and myself in years past. This, I could do.

On a winter day in June, Gene and I traveled to Zwelitsha in the Ciskei, a homeland for the Xhosa people. We had one sewing machine in the back seat. Pastor Albert Masetti met us in the church yard. As we entered the church, I observed nine warmly dressed women. One lady had her baby tied to her back. Sounds of Xhosa echoed in my ears. I had never studied Xhosa, and I wondered how we would manage with the pastor translating, both in the sewing class and the Bible study.

Earlier I had cut out ten aprons for the sewing class since I knew the church wouldn't have a large cutting table. Sewing items—scissors, needles, thread, and fabric—were expensive, and the women would need help with start-up supplies.

It was a delight to watch the women's faces as they sewed on a machine for the first time. Most made good progress. They were happy and proud. Even though manual labor had roughened their hands, they succeeded at the finer skill of sewing. With only one machine, the women didn't finish their aprons, but they would continue sewing them by hand at home.

I had learned that the Black people were more event-oriented than time conscious. As I remembered this, I scheduled the sewing class first and the Bible study second. I hoped for a good turnout. The ladies began drifting in at different times, mostly after the scheduled time. It became a personal learning curve throughout my time in South Africa since I was time conscious.

Before leaving, I gave each woman a long piece of string. For the next class, they were to bring three lengths of string: one to represent the length of the shoulder to the waist, another for the size of the waist, and the last for the dress length. These measurements would be used to sew pinafores for their little girls.

Upon returning home, I wondered how to proceed with this new ministry. First-City Church in East London had invited me to speak at their mission program. I used that engagement to share the needs of the sewing classes.

A week later, Gene and I drove to Zwelitsha for another class. This time, we loaded the car with a sewing machine, fabric, thread, and newsprint pinafore patterns that I had cut out. On that cold winter morning, I couldn't help but think the sewing class attendance would be low since there was no heat in the church building.

As we drove into the churchyard, we saw the pastor walking from the manse. He came to greet us. Gene called, "Good morning, Albert. How are you?"

We appreciated that he spoke English with our limited knowledge of the Xhosa language and of the customs and manners of the people. In the past, I had been one to go where angels feared to tread. I certainly felt that way now.

Inside the vestibule, I heard the hum of Xhosa clicks and laughter from a group of ladies sitting at the front. To my delight, all nine women had returned, including a lady with her baby. I felt strange greeting them since they didn't speak English.

However, they came prepared with the string measurements I had requested. One woman had ingeniously made three knots in a long string that represented the measurements for her little girl.

"Good!" I smiled at her.

Proudly, the woman smiled back. I proceeded to call out the measurements of each woman's strings. Adelaide, the pastor's wife, wrote them down. We then moved to the next step: cutting out the pattern from the fabric. One by one, each woman laid fabric on the platform beside the pulpit and cut out the pinafore pattern. They had to stoop or kneel on the floor to accomplish this task.

Albert placed the sewing machine on the altar table with a chair in front. With the nine ladies in a semicircle, I showed them how to make the gathered hem for the skirt ruffle and how to thread the machine. They did well gathering the stitches but struggled when they tried to hold the fabric pieces in place with one hand and crank the machine handle with the other. I had worried how the ladies would manage this task, but they showed determination and perseverance. Before the class ended, each woman had a turn at the machine, and in time, they would finish their pinafores in a later class.

Afterwards, we assembled for the Bible study. Standing beside the pastor, I would speak a sentence, and he translated it into Xhosa. The Bible study dealt with stewardship of time, talents, gifts, and money.

On another winter day, Gene went back to see Albert, and on his way out of Zwelitsha, he had to stop for a man to crawl across the street because he had no feet. The man wore small pads on his knees made from a tire for protection. As he worked to cross, Gene witnessed anguish and fear on the man's face. He was thinly clad with a tattered coat. Gene and I felt overwhelming sorrow for this man, and desperately wanted to help. This heart-wrenching sight would cause us to seek new avenues to minister to the impoverished people.

The sewing ministry continued in other places. One afternoon, Lionel Grunewald drove us to the village of Keiskammahoek to deliver a sewing machine. The drive took two hours. When we arrived, fifteen ladies had assembled. Gene demonstrated how the machine worked, how to thread it, and how to fill the bobbin.

I later met with Angelina Lata, the pastor's wife. I was so thrilled that she spoke English. I thought it would be wiser to teach her sewing skills than try to teach the ladies through an interpreter. I showed her how to make an apron and encouraged her to finish in my absence. I also promised to return later for a full day's lesson on how to make a dress.

Two weeks later, I met with Angelina and a high school English teacher in the church hall. With the fabric already pre-cut, Angelina began stitching up the dress pieces. Since the machine didn't have the proper attachment for insertion of a zipper, she sewed it by hand.

A month later, Gene and I returned to check on Angelina. We met her in the church hall where she had set up the sewing machine. Soon Joy and Joyce, her twin daughters, came in from school. Wearing gold blouses and green jumpers, they looked lovely in their uniforms. Sadly, in times past, superstitious Xhosa members would kill one or both babies that were born as twins. I was thankful these girls stood before me.

The highlight of my day came when Angelina showed me a black church uniform with a lovely wide and white collar. Earlier, I had made her a pattern from her old church uniform. She took that pattern, and with only two classes, had sewn her own new uniform. It was a joy to see her progress. Sometimes women would wear their church uniforms to their ladies' meetings or to church.

During our ministry, we needed eye exams. On October 27, 1988, I wrote the following to my children in a form letter:

After we left the doctor's office, we went out to the car. As your daddy unlocked my car door, a Xhosa lady came up to me to ask for a job. I told her I had a maid. (As you know I got one for one day a week to stop the flow of people to my door asking for a maid's job.) Anyway, back to my story, I gave her R2,00($1.00) from my purse as I knew or rather thought the next question would be for food. I gave her a tract in Xhosa. She *was more interested in the tract. As we backed out into the street, I turned back to see what she did with the tract. She had sat down on a low wall to read the tract. She seemed engrossed in it. I prayed for her that if she was not a Christian, she would be saved reading that tract. That was the highlight of my day.*

I had a similar experience the day before at my front door. I had given a lady bread and a Xhosa tract. From my living room window, I watched her reading it as she walked up the street. I do hope our lives are making a difference here. At times, we feel most frustrated at not being able to speak Xhosa. Our formal classes for it will start in January which is none too soon for us.

A while later, I returned to Zwelitsha. I marveled at the finished items that the ladies had sewn. Seeing their happy faces thrilled my heart and reassured me that I had made a difference in their lives, both financially and spiritually. However, teaching them about the love of Jesus always remained the highlight of my ministry. The Lord took the little I had achieved with the ladies and blessed it many times over.

Wherever I looked, I saw people struggling. They were hungry, poor, and defeated. They stood in the streets, the byways, the shops, the fields, the villages—everywhere. How they needed help, hope and love. How they needed Jesus as Lord and Savior. But the little I did only seemed like a drop in this ocean of human suffering.

Chapter Five

CHALUMNA

*Create in me a pure heart, O God,
and renew a steadfast spirit within me.
Psalm 51:10*

On a winter morning, we traveled to Chalumna to deliver a sewing machine, fabric, Bibles, and literature for the pastor. When Gene inquired about the pastor, Ivy, the pastor's wife, reported that he was in the hospital. He had taken a fall three years earlier, which caused a disc to slip in his back and at times, resulted in paralysis. Ivy also had a chronic ulcer on the calf of her leg that wouldn't heal. She'd had it for ten years and could no longer afford the expensive ointment.

Sadly, we heard that Ivy's husband died on August 4, the weekend before our next sewing class. We traveled to the manse and found ten women with Ivy who sat on a mat, depicting her mourning status. For a month, she would sleep on the mat. According to Xhosa culture, she would also wear black as a new widow for a month. She scheduled her husband's funeral for August 16.

Later, I returned for the sewing class at Chalumna and traveled alone. When I reached the manse, I saw the sewing machine on a table. We could not meet in the church because the teachers held school there. During our class, the women shared disturbing news.

One lady reported, "A boycott is going on in East London. Our people will not allow us to go into any White store. The man who owns a store in Chalumna went into a store in East London. He was seen. As a result, he was beaten up and his truck (bakkie) destroyed."

Ivy added, "Now Chalumna is without a store. The people are too poor to go to Mdantsane for groceries or to Bisho, which is even further." Mdantsane was a township of a million people in the Ciskei near East London, and Bisho was its capital.

Another lady said, "People are out of gas for cooking. There is no electricity in the village. They are out of matches and corn meal too."

In addition to the boycott in East London, there was constant unrest in the country. I wrote the following in a letter to our friends, Tommy and Gloria Brown, on August 8, 1989: *We hear of more bombs going off. Unless God intervenes in a miraculous way, I don't see how this country can avoid bloodshed in its future. Whenever we travel, we take our passports in the event of a national emergency and have been advised by our Mission to submit an escape route. I think our only course would be to take a boat as people would flock to Johannesburg trying to get out. People are immigrating to Canada, Australia, and other places already."*

As I thought about the unrest in the country, I gazed at the ladies and wondered what their future would look like. While one lady sewed a dress, others sat on the floor and positioned crocheted squares together. Talking among themselves, they discussed who was going to get my necklace in the event of my departure.

When I packed up to leave, a lady asked for a ride. I welcomed her because I wouldn't be traveling alone to East London. About halfway, we reached her destination, and I tried not to worry for the remainder of the trip.

Despite the growing tension, I continued with sewing classes in Chalumna. On one occasion, the hand-cranked sewing machine wouldn't work properly. But the ten ladies sat on the floor, delighted to sew a quilt top together.

On another day, I returned to Chalumna in a drizzle of rain and knew some wouldn't be able to come. When I parked in front of the manse, a lady helped me carry in the sewing machine because I had taken it home to clean out the clogged thread. I walked into the darkened living room and saw one small window. They had no electricity, and the door was closed due to the cold weather.

The ladies sewed the dark red and black print fabric with black thread. I asked one of the ladies to thread the needle as I couldn't see in the darkness. I'd taken Xhosa tracts to give to the ladies to use in witnessing. For a while, we talked about the information in the tract. While I waited for the ladies to finish sewing, Ivy helped me with my Xhosa.

When they completed their sewing for the day, I gave my personal testimony because they had been asking questions about me. They gave me the name of "Nosapho" meaning "family mother." Usually ten ladies came, but on this rainy day, we only had four.

In a letter to my daughter on September 28, 1989, I wrote:

I wonder if you heard about the big march that was held in East London yesterday. There were about 40,000 people who attended it, the largest one of its kind in South Africa. It was peaceful. Our maid and gardener had to leave by 12:00 p.m. as they wouldn't be able to get transportation past then. As it was, they were too late, and Daddy had to take them to the township of Mdantsane. Yesterday was the first day I have actually felt fear for the situation in South Africa. It has always been far removed from us.

A pastor at Adelaide has been told by the "Comrades" (Communists) that he is a marked man since he does not participate in their activity. They threatened him with the necklace. He is planning to go talk to one of them and explain why he does not participate.

At Duncan Village where I went today for a sewing class, the pastor was asked to attend the march yesterday. He left the village like he was going to the march and then went elsewhere.

The boycott of the East London stores began on September 13, and it would last until October 13. Each time I traveled to Chalumna, I heard bad news from the ladies, and I felt great empathy for them.

During my trek to Chalumna on December 19, which I hoped would be the last sewing class for a while, I planned a Christmas party and took cake, tea, sugar and cream. During teatime, the ladies showed me the quilt they had sewed together. They had done well matching the corners and designs.

Unexpectedly, the BWA president came in with a big bouquet of white lilies, took my hand, and kissed it. She gave me the lilies and a hand-woven rug she had made. Another seamstress presented me with a woven tray she had made. Gene commented to me later, "I don't think you'll ever see a better expression of love." I felt much appreciated and honored.

In the late summer, I held another class in Chalumna. Since the coup in the Ciskei, Gene went with me and planned to prepare a sermon while I conducted the class. Usually he sat in the car, but on this day, it was too hot. When we drove up, we saw two ladies sitting on a bench in the shade by the side of the house. I suggested he take their place because they had come to greet us and help carry things in. He came in, greeted the ladies, and then left. I forgot to bring scissors, and Maureen, the lady who wanted me to show her how to make a blouse, went to her house to get her scissors, which didn't take long since she lived nearby.

I was relieved to see that they had ironed the thin, flimsy material which can be tough to sew. Unfortunately, the blades of Maureen's scissors were less than two inches long. Cutting took longer, and flies hummed as the humidity soared.

After an hour, I went to see Gene for a short break. As I walked out, I felt the cool breeze from the ocean and saw him sitting in the quiet and coolness, his Bible and notebook in hand. At that moment, Satan came and taunted me, "See how easy he has it." In my irritable state, I repeated those evil words to Gene.

Of course, Gene didn't like what I said, and I didn't feel good about myself for blurting those words out. After that, my interactions with the sewing class and with Gene went downhill the rest of the day, and time dragged on. About one o'clock, a lady served me a small glass of soda pop. At times, I would take bread, cake, or rolls to my sewing classes, but this time I didn't take anything. I soon had a headache, an unhappy husband, and an unhappy self.

Later, I learned the ladies noticed I was troubled. One cannot fool an African national, and there was no need to try. Previously, they had requested that I bring yarn to the class.

On this occasion, I also brought some unfinished knitting pieces which had been donated. One lady started unraveling a knitted piece without taking any precaution to keep it from tangling. I took her yarn and showed the ladies how to wrap it around my arm, leaving a big loop. I then laid the loop on the table and tied it in three different places with small lengths of yarn. To get rid of the wrinkles, I soaked it in water, wrung it, and hung it on the back of a chair to dry. The ladies could wrap it in a ball after it dried.

Next, I noticed one lady had her blouse completely cut out. We set up the sewing machine. The two interfacings were to be sewn on the two front sections of the blouse. The sewing machine would normally knot the bobbin thread in a majestic way, making spirals like spider webs. But after a while, I decided that it was too much to struggle with. I also noticed the lady had sewn on one of the interfacings incorrectly. I don't know if she switched it when I went out to moan at Gene again or not.

By that time, though, Ivy told me the ladies had observed that I wasn't cheerful, and I told her I didn't sleep well. I don't know if they understood or not. Right before I prepared to leave, Ivy asked me to pray for the ladies. They began to put their shawls and coats on, and someone closed the door as was their custom. I made a pretense of praying. How I disliked praying when I was out of kilter with the Lord, Gene, or myself. After my empty prayer, Gene and I had a cold ride home.

But I knew what I needed to do to make things right. Like David the Psalmist wrote about in Psalm 51:10, I wanted "a pure heart" and a renewed spirit. I apologized to Gene, who readily accepted my apology. I asked the Lord to forgive me, but I struggled to forgive myself. However, by God's grace, I would return to Chalumna with a renewed spirit.

CHAPTER SIX

EASTER WEEKEND

*That I might know him and the power of his resurrection,
and share his sufferings, becoming like him in his death,
that by any means possible I may attain the resurrection
from the dead.*
Philippians 3:10-11

On a pleasant day in March, we drove to Braelyn, an Indian village near East London. Pastor David Governor and his wife Pat had permission to use a friend's garage for a Good Friday worship service. It would be a time of reflection and a focus on Christ's sacrificial death for the sins of mankind.

When we arrived, we saw David's father and cousin removing pine pews from the back garage wall and arranging them. Pat was pouring grape juice into communion cups as Ryan, her three-year-old son, watched.

David and Pat had arrived in Braelyn in July of 1988, six months after we arrived in East London. Seeing their new church plant within the Indian community reminded me of our time ministering to Native Americans in New Mexico. A few people shouldered most of the work with hopes of developing a viable church. I easily understood their frustration, especially after hearing that they had previously lived in the city of Durban, located on South Africa's east side. Durban was home to a large Indian population, where the Christian work was much more developed.

On this noisy Friday with dogs barking, cars driving by, and someone using a chainsaw, we began singing the appropriate hymn, "Man of Sorrows." Since there were no musical instruments, we sang a cappella. After more songs, Rowan, the Governors' eleven-year-old son, passed around a small bowl for the offering. David then gave the message and ended the service with the Lord's Supper.

While David took some attendees home, Gene and I helped gather songbooks, collect the offering, and restack the pews so the garage owner could park his van inside. Next, we drove to the Governors' third floor apartment for dinner. David had placed their name on a waiting list for a house with hopes of improving their living conditions and ability to minister to the community.

During dinner, we heard more about the family's plight. David shared that a teacher had kicked Rowan a month after they arrived in East London and that the abusive behavior had occurred several times. I was appalled. David also told us of his continued search for a job that would provide for his family. Thankfully, Pat had a part-time job. We would continue to see David and Pat in meetings throughout our time in East London.

Back home, we were cleaning the breakfast dishes Saturday morning when the telephone rang. Gene answered it. Shortly, he returned and softly said, "It's Maretta, and she's called to tell you that your mother died yesterday."

I was sad, but thankful she wasn't suffering anymore. Earlier in the year, my mother had endured two bouts of pneumonia, and we didn't know if she would make it. She also had struggled with Alzheimer's for many long and arduous years. Now, Good Friday, the day she died, was her homecoming day.

I dreaded talking to my sister. I knew she would want me to return for the funeral, which would be in Greenville, Alabama. I had previously told Ada Sue, my sister-in-law, that I wanted to know when Mother died so I could be present at her funeral. But now the logistics were much more difficult. Due to economic sanctions, we could only fly out of South Africa on KLM, the Dutch Airlines, on Tuesdays and Fridays. I would then fly to the Netherlands and on to New York and finally, Montgomery, Alabama. I was torn. I wanted to be there, but my delayed travels would postpone the funeral. Further, I didn't sense the Lord was leading me to return.

I picked up the phone. "I want to come, Maretta, but I don't feel I can."

Maretta quickly responded, "Are you sure you won't regret this?"

We talked a while longer. What I didn't tell her was that I feared traveling without Gene and going through New York City. But the thought of not being with my family also brought sadness.

On Easter morning, I called our son David and learned that our three children planned to attend their grandmother's funeral. This added new stress and pressure. I began to doubt my decision. If I went, I would have the opportunity to see my extended family and all my children. But I still believed the Lord was saying no.

After the phone conversation, I talked with Gene. Sensing my uncertainty, he responded, "You made the right decision."

Just a few minutes later, a gentleman from King Williams Town called. I heard Gene express deep sympathy. When he hung up, he told me a young man named Darryl had been killed in a car accident. Darryl was the middle son of Peter and Joan Fourie, who lived in Breidbach, a Colored community forty-five minutes from East London.

Darryl was only eighteen years old.

The news chilled my heart. My mind raced back to a June morning in 1954 when I was at Shocco Springs Camp in Alabama for a Bible drill. Around 4:00 a.m., a woman came to the room where I bunked with my roommate. She turned on the light and asked, "Which one of you is Ellamae Thompson?"

Learning I was the one, she came and sat down beside me. "Something bad has happened, and you're going to have to go home. Your brother drowned last night. Your cousins are here to take you home." I couldn't believe her words, nor could I cry. I was in shock. She helped me pack my clothes. I told my roommate goodbye and left.

Outside, I saw my cousins, Wilbur and Elmore Thompson, standing under the streetlight beside the car. On the ride home, I couldn't sleep. My thoughts tumbled about. It seemed like I was living a nightmare, but it also felt real. I dreaded going home. I was now the oldest child. I thought the world should stand still since Everett wasn't with us anymore. And now he wouldn't be coming home from college the following weekend when I returned from camp. How could this tragedy have happened to my family?

Everett was only eighteen years old.

Seven summers earlier in 1947, Everett and I had attended the morning revival service at Ebenezer East Baptist Church near Greenville, Alabama. I could easily remember the pastor standing by the altar. He invited those who wanted to place their faith and trust in Jesus as Savior and Lord to come forward. The Holy Spirit tugged at my heart, and I knew the Lord was inviting me to come and follow Him. I left the second pew where I stood and walked toward the pastor. As the congregation continued to sing, the pastor counseled me. Standing nearby, I saw Everett waiting to speak to the pastor. He, too, wanted to make the same decision.

On Friday morning, Everett and I were baptized at a local pond with six other new believers. He and I were close growing up together, and it thrilled me that we had become Christians in the same service and baptized at the same time. As each baptismal candidate was baptized, the pastor spoke the words, "I baptize you in the name of the Father, and of the Son, and of the Holy Spirit." My baptism was a symbolic act and did not save me. The old person was buried with Jesus in death and raised to a new life in Him. It was a wonderful and amazing day.

That memory of our baptism faded when I arrived home and saw my grief-stricken parents. I hurt more for them than I did for myself. They had come face-to-face with a parent's worst nightmare—the death of a child. They were inconsolable, even though they knew Everett was in the presence of Jesus.

Now, in 1989, my thoughts turned to Peter and Joan. Gene was preaching the Easter service at their church. I tried to prepare myself to face them. On Sunday, we drove to the school in Breidbach where the service was held. Waiting outside the classroom, we saw Peter and Joan drive up. I saw on their faces the same horrendous grief that I had witnessed on my parents' faces. It was 1954 all over again.

The service began with a time of singing and worship. I sat at a desk by the window. Joan sat across from me in the next aisle. We sang "What a Friend We Have in Jesus." That hymn had been sung at my father's funeral after his tractor accident in 1980. And now my mother had just died. I was so choked up that I could only sing two lines. But the words of the last verse spoke to me, *In His arms He'll take and shield thee, Thou wilt find a solace there.* I felt as though the Lord Himself was holding me and giving me peace and comfort.

We went on to sing "It is Well with My Soul." Through tears, Joan looked at the words in her songbook while the congregation sang. My heart broke for her. I knew she and Peter would need to grieve this profound loss, and that their lives would be forever changed. Darryl would never marry, have children or attend family celebrations or holidays.

But I also knew that time would help these grief-stricken parents, that they would learn to live again without their son. And I knew that God was good (Psalm 34:8) and that He would work this tragedy out for good (Romans 8:28). I had witnessed these truths in my own life.

Gene got up to preach. He spoke from 1 Corinthian 15:1-19. He reminded us that Easter, the celebration of the resurrection of Jesus, proved that truth was stronger than falsehood, good was stronger than evil, love was stronger than hate, and life was stronger than death. Good Friday was an unimaginable horror for Jesus, but three days later, angels declared: "He is not here; He has risen!" (Luke 24:6).

And therein lies our hope.

Joan and Peter would see Darryl again. I would see Everett and my father and my mother again. But in this life, the words of Philippians 3:10-11 ring true. We seek to know Christ and the power of his resurrection. We share in his suffering, becoming like Him in His death, that we may attain the resurrection from the dead.

CHAPTER SEVEN

OUT OF RUINS

*O Lord, you are my God: You have been a refuge
for the poor, a refuge for the needy in his distress,
a shelter from the storm and a shade from the heat.
Isaiah 25:4*

One day in July, Gene and I met Peter Mabena at a service station in East London. Peter had invited Gene to preach in his church, Mashologu Baptist Church, in Duncan Village. At the time, it was not safe for a White person to enter this city of 80,000 unless escorted by a well-respected Black man.

We followed Peter in our car. He parked at a Catholic church where his church held services. Only a few people were present for the morning services. In the room next door, I could hear the Methodist congregation singing.

After the service, Gene and I walked a short distance with Peter to the original site of Mashologu Baptist Church. We smelled food cooking from the nearby shacks and lean-tos.

About three hundred people lived in the immediate area. Our eyes stung from the haze of smoke that settled over the area.

Many years before, the government had planned to relocate Duncan Village. They thought it was too close to East London. To accommodate their plan, they bought several church buildings, including Mashologu Baptist Church. During the time the church sat vacant, people stripped the wood from the floors and the ceiling, and knocked out the Palladian windows. Only the ruins of stone walls and the roof remained. As time passed, squatters settled on the grounds, and after many years, the government left the location of the city unchanged.

As we walked to the old church site, I saw children playing in the sand. One little boy was naked, his stomach extended. I knew this was evidence of malnutrition, but I soon learned that the Black people here were better off compared to those in other African countries.

Peter had heard the government planned to release the four church sites in Duncan Village. Thirty-one churches applied for the Mashologu Baptist Church site. As the officials decided who would receive the building, many people started praying.

In July, the mayor's office called to inform Peter that his church had been granted the church site. Overjoyed, Peter made a trip to the mayor's office to ask if it was really true. Then he came to our home to give us the good news. I loved hearing him say, "I am happy."

After installation of a cement floor, windows, and pews, the congregation began to worship once again in their beloved sanctuary. It was especially meaningful to Peter and his wife Oscarina. Their wedding had taken place in this lovely church building before the government intervened.

In September, American pastors arrived to help with revivals in South African Baptist churches. Gene was asked to help since the demand was great. On Sunday night, Peter's church could not have services because there was no electricity in his part of the village, but he was hoping to get lanterns. Happily, a man from a White church provided a generator, since the Mashologu church was wired for electricity. As Gene and I drove up that night, I will never forget the site of the lit sanctuary. The church glowed with beauty.

On the last night of the revival, while Gene preached and Peter interpreted, we had something of a fright. There was a loud noise that sounded like a gunshot. I looked at Oscarina sitting next to me, and Peter, standing beside Gene. They were perfectly composed. It was then I knew not to panic even when the loud noise happened again. Afterwards, I learned that the boys who were disciplined during the service had gone outside. They took revenge by throwing rocks at the building. Oscarina had worried they might break the windows. Thankfully, that didn't happen.

As time passed and with the church overcoming tremendous odds, I saw the ministries of the Mashologu church gaining momentum in Duncan Village. Oscarina asked me to help start a sewing ministry with Bible classes.

The first time I arrived for the sewing class, thirteen ladies were present. In addition to the sewing lesson and the Bible class, I gave out tracts in Xhosa and offered a Bible to those who didn't have one. I noticed a lady in the front row who had extra-large legs. I wondered if she had congestive heart failure. When I later talked with Oscarina, she told me the lady died two days after that first sewing class. Since the lady was new to the group, Oscarina didn't know if she was a Christian. How I pray the lady had an opportunity to know Jesus loved her and died for her.

Our time of ministering in South Africa brought a keen awareness of the mortality of life. We felt an urgency to share the gospel and to help those in need. As I conducted the sewing classes in Duncan Village, Gene and Peter visited the people who lived nearby and shared Christ with them. Many received Jesus as Lord and Savior. I loved hearing about their conversions and seeing how their faces glowed with joy. Further, while my sewing class occupied the front of the church, Oscarina's foster daughter, Tanya, taught kindergarten classes at the back of the church.

During one sewing class, Oscarina apologized for the poor attendance. Only four ladies were present. I told her not to worry. Each lady would have her own sewing machine since I had brought four. But after we began the Bible class, ladies kept coming in. As Oscarina translated my words into Xhosa,

I wondered how I would teach the sewing class. By the end of the study, I counted twenty-seven ladies! Oscarina told me they had been looking forward to the class. They were eager to come and learn.

Even with only four sewing machines, the class turned out well. As in classes I had conducted in other towns, the ladies cut out fabric on the cement platform of the sanctuary. They also took turns sewing. One woman named Vesta sewed with gnarled hands and thick glasses. She was able to guide two pieces of fabric under the needle with her left hand and turn the handle of the sewing machine with her right one. I admired her determination. By the end of class, four ladies had finished their aprons, and many had begun sewing theirs. The ladies glowed when Oscarina praised them for their progress. She hoped they would be able to sell their items to help their families.

I commented to her, "You surely must get discouraged at times seeing great need daily. Wherever I drive here, I see such poverty."

"Yes," she said. "When we look around at the needs of the people, we get discouraged, but when we look up to the Lord, we get encouraged. And that is why we are able to carry on."

And carry on she did. Oscarina and her family of six lived in the two rooms of the vestry adjacent to the back of the church. The first room served as a living room, children's bedroom, and kitchen. Sometimes, she also fed seniors in this room. Having only one kerosene heater, she boiled the water to make tea *and* to cook food. Like a thoroughfare, her home provided a warm spirit of hospitality to whomever entered. Eventually, a manse was built on the church grounds and the Mabena family moved in.

It was amazing to watch the progress of the Mashologu church. Many, many people came to salvation. Peter, Oscarina, and their family continued to be faithful to the Mashologu church, and the Lord blessed them abundantly.

What was once ruins in a desperate wasteland became a vibrant sanctuary, flowing with streams of love and hope.

Chapter Eight

A CHRISTMAS MEMORY

But the angel said to them, "Do not be afraid, for behold, I bring you good tidings of great joy which will be to all people. For there is born to you this day in the city of David a Savior, who is Christ the Lord."
Luke 2:10-11

On a November day, the sun streamed through the windows as warm breezes ruffled my living room and dining room drapes. I had looked forward to this morning because the ladies from my church were coming to my house for our Christmas program.

I thought of the Christmases spent with my family back in New Mexico. Thinking of them made me sad because I missed them and regretted that I was not with them on Christmas. Since I had lived near the Rocky Mountains, we would experience frigid nights. When we went caroling, we bundled up in coats, hats, boots, and gloves, and people served us hot chocolate. But Christmas in South Africa meant going to the beach and singing Christmas carols in the nearby parks while wearing light clothing. Living in the southern hemisphere made such a difference!

As my second Christmas approached, I found myself excited. I had adapted to my new home. Eager to decorate, I hung our family stockings by the mantel leaving a space for my new grandson Caleb's stocking, not yet finished. I sewed and stuffed cut-out nativity figures to adorn the piano. Red flowers and a candelabra brightened my dining table. Gene had tied two Christmas trees together to make it "prettier." (If South Africans had a tree, it was usually small.) With perspiration running down his face and the ceiling fan on full blast, he chuckled as he hung "icicles" on the tree.

Earlier that morning, I had unwrapped my glass nativity set to place on a round table in the guest room. I searched and searched through the box for baby Jesus, but to no avail. Baby Jesus was missing.

With the ding-dong of the doorbell, I hurried to answer the door and invited the ladies in.

Looking around the room, Denise said, "It looks like Christmas. I can't believe Christmas is only a month away."

"Oh, how this year has flown," chimed Gwenda, "and I'm not ready for Christmas."

"Ellamae, your tree is so lovely," Jeannie, our pastor's wife, said while reading and looking at the ornaments.

We chatted and soon enjoyed teatime with the goodies they had brought. Afterwards, we moved to the living room and started our meeting with a prayer time. Since I was in charge of the program, I planned to share a story from the December 1988 *Guideposts* magazine. During World War I, the Christmas Truce of 1914 took place in the trenches on the Western Front. Along with the story, I would also include the background of a few Christmas carols.

Immediately after I finished, a dear little English lady named Mary said, "I was born on May 13, 1914, and my father went off to war right after my birth. The next time I saw my father was at Christmastime in 1918 when the war was over. I couldn't understand why this strange man should come into our home and sit at the head of the table and sleep in the bed with our mother where my brother and I had been sleeping."

"I never knew that story about you, Mary," Sharon said.

A quiet stillness settled over us. I wondered if the ladies thought about Mary's story the way I did. I recalled my parents being together for all my Christmases as a child. Truly, war cut deeply, broke families, and destroyed peace. Mary and countless others suffered.

After the ladies left, I went back to look for baby Jesus again. Only when I turned over the glass manger did I find Him on the underside. I had placed the manger upside down. The Prince of Peace was there all the time.

Man-made peace is fleeting. For a few precious hours, peace reigned between enemies on Christmas Day in 1914, but sadly, World War I would not end until 1918. Other wars would scar the twentieth century—World War II, the Korean War, the Vietnam War. Even the fall of the Berlin Wall on November 9, 1989, just three weeks prior, would not ensure lasting "peace on earth."

That job belongs to One and Only One:

> *For to us a Child is born, to us a Son is given;*
>
> *and the government shall be upon His*
>
> *shoulder, and His name shall be called*
>
> *Wonderful Counselor,*
>
> *Mighty God,*
>
> *Everlasting Father,*
>
> ***Prince of Peace.***
>
> Isaiah 9:6
>
> **JESUS**

CHAPTER NINE

NELSON MANDELA

I looked for a man among them who would build up
the wall and stand before me in the gap.
Ezekiel 22:30

"As I walked out the door toward the gate that would lead to my freedom, I knew if I didn't leave my bitterness and hatred behind, I'd still be in prison."[2] The man who coined these words had been incarcerated for twenty-seven years. On February 11, 1990, Gene and I watched on national television as Nelson Mandela walked into freedom. Staying behind bars for so long crafted him a hero to the people.

For some time, the government had worked to acquire a release for him. As the government continued on this track, he was taken to a cottage on the grounds of Victor Verster Prison

---

[2] Tayo Rockson, "*What Nelson Mandela Taught Us About Seeing the Bigger Picture,*" tayorockson.com, 2021.

to learn how to enter society again.[3] Officials would take him to a café for tea. He would take walks on the beach. Nobody recognized him because his black hair had turned gray, and wrinkles etched his face.

Mandela was born Rolihlahla Mandela on July 18, 1918, at Mvezo, Transkei, South Africa. On his first day of school, his teacher gave each student an English name, and she named Rolihlaha "Nelson." He received a British education. Growing up, he dreamed about what contributions he could make to the freedom struggle for his people.[4]

Mandela was baptized into the Methodist Church. As a member of the Students Christian Association, he taught Bible studies in the neighboring villages. On Sundays, he taught a Bible class at church.[5] He received his higher education at the University College at Ft. Hare and the University of Witwatersrand in Johannesburg, where he studied law.[6]

To help the people who suffered under apartheid, Mandela joined the African National Congress (ANC), "a social-democratic and political party." He wanted to participate in the struggle for racial equality and later became the leader of the resistance to apartheid. However, in 1960, the

---

[3] Nelson Mandela, *Long Walk to Freedom* (New York, Little, Brown and Company, 2013), p. 543.

[4] Nelsonmandela.org, Mandela Archives, *Biography and Timeline*, 2024.

[5] Michael Trimmer, *Nelson Mandela and His Faith*, christianitytoday.com, December 10, 2013

[6] Nelsonmandela.org, Mandela Archives, *Biography and Timeline*, 2024.

government banned the ANC.[7] When this happened, many members went into exile, but still worked for the party.

In the Rivonia Trial, Mandela and those arrested with him decided they wouldn't testify as witnesses or submit to cross-examination. They also decided that Mandela would give a speech from the dock. In his speech, he would put the state on trial. A quote from his speech read, "I have cherished the ideal of a democratic and free society in which all persons live together in harmony and with equal opportunities. It is an ideal which I hope to live for and to achieve. But if needs be, it is an ideal for which I am prepared to die." [8]

On Friday, June 12, 1964, Mandela along with seven others were sentenced to life imprisonment. They were taken to Robben Island Prison, six miles from Cape Town. There, he worked in the lime quarry and endured hard labor and solitary confinement. He was allowed one letter and one visitor every six months. In 1982, he was transferred to Pollsmoor Prison in Cape Town.[9]

In November 1985, the National Party Government entered into secret negotiations with Mandela for what both parties hoped might lead to an ultimate transition to a multi-racial government.[10]

---

[7] Britannica.com, *African National Congress*, September 21, 2024.
[8] Douglas O. Linder, *The Nelson Mandela (Rivonia) Trial: An Account*, famous-trials.com, 1995-2024.
[9] Nelsonmandela.org, Mandela Archives, *Biography and Timeline*, 2024.
[10] Michael Parks, *Proposal Would Form Multiracial Government in South Africa Province*, latimes.com, November 29, 1986.

After his release from prison, Mandela entered passionately into his life's work. He wanted to accomplish the goals he and others had formulated decades earlier. At his first ANC conference in 1990, he was elected president.[11]

In 1993, I heard on television that Mandela received the Nobel Prize for Peace along with South Africa's president at the time, F. W. de Klerk. Together, the two men forged the transition from apartheid to a multiracial democracy.

In 1994, in the first democratic presidential election, Nelson Mandela became the first Black president of South Africa. His inauguration took place in Pretoria.

Mandela gave his life to fulfill the mission of seeing oppressed races free from living under the apartheid system. His efforts to end apartheid and to lead people of different races toward reconciliation inspired the world.

Mandela was the man for this long dark hour in South Africa's history.

---

[11] Nelsonmandela.org, Mandela Archives, *Biography and Timeline*, 2024.

Chapter Ten

COUP IN THE CISKEI

*When He (Jesus) saw the crowds, He felt compassion
for them, because they were weary and worn out,
like sheep without a shepherd.
Matthew 9:36*

During the weekend before my birthday, we went to a lovely hotel beside the Indian Ocean an hour and a half drive from East London. We would provide childcare for the workers of the Kei Mission (formerly Transkei Mission) during their prayer retreat. Ten children, ranging from two to eleven years of age, were our responsibility for the weekend. A thirteen-year-old, who was a guest at the hotel, joined us for the sessions as well. I loved the challenge the children presented and enjoyed the little girls who satisfied my need for my little granddaughters.

While we had our teatime on Sunday Morning, Rue Scott, a lecturer at the Baptist International Theological Seminary near Dimbasa, said to Gene, "There's been an attempted coup in the Ciskei."

"What happened?" Gene asked.

"I don't know. That's all I've heard so far."

Someone called Radio South Africa. They confirmed the coup was a success. When we learned this news, we were not surprised since we'd heard reports of dissatisfaction with the Ciskei government for some time. When the coup happened, we were in a safe place by the seaside.

Driving back that afternoon, we wondered what we would find. Would we be able to get into our community and home? Mdantsane was a mere twenty-minute drive from our house. Would people be walking to our area? These thoughts permeated our minds. When we arrived, we learned that the Ciskei was in a general state of anarchy like a classroom without a teacher.

Not long afterwards, the telephone rang. It was Dot Ditty, a colleague from Johannesburg. She said, "I told Jim that I bet Ellamae was scared and wished she could get out of the country."

"Actually, Dot," I replied, "it has brought out feelings to the contrary in me. I don't want to leave the people or walk out of trouble." I requested that she pray that Gene and I would appropriate the peace of God in our lives and take away our fear, which He did on that day. (Answered prayer is amazing!)

Ron Lomax, a colleague from Bophuthatswana, called later in the afternoon. Since I was the prayer chairman for our company, he asked for prayer. He had been tear-gassed as he helped a baby, who had also been tear-gassed. He told us that it was quite painful, and he couldn't see. He was also afraid.

We soon learned the details of the military coup. Brigadier General Oupa of the Ciskei army and his soldiers took control while the President-for-life Lennox Sebe visited Taiwan. Immediately, rioting and looting broke out that targeted stores, government offices, and homes.

The government had designated the Ciskei a homeland in 1983, but no other country had ever recognized it as an independent country except South Africa. At the request of Brigadier General Oupa, South Africa sent troops in to quell the mobs.

During the thirty-six hours of anarchy, the police reported seventy burned factories that resulted in 18,000 jobs lost. The mobs also burned buses that provided transportation for their own people.

A pastor from Mdantsane said there wasn't a shop left unscathed. Further, the coup left twenty dead and more than 200 injured. Hospitals suffered an acute blood shortage, and scores of young people were admitted for severe alcoholic intoxication.

Gene called the pastors in Zwelitsha, Duncan Village, and Bisho. He learned that church members had stayed away from the rioting. Also, the pastors told Gene that troops had sealed off the borders and cautioned him not to travel in the area for the time being. We had to cancel our weekly visits into Duncan Village for my sewing and Bible classes and Gene's evangelism class with the pastor. A scheduled trip to take sixty-five mattresses to a Ciskei tent camp of 1,000 refugees was also postponed.

Following the coup, young people came to the homes of the pastors in the Ciskei to enlist their children in looting and burning. When the pastors' children refused, the young people threatened to burn *their* homes, viewing them as enemies.

The African National Congress seemed to be responsible for much unrest in our area. Many trucks and buses loaded with cheering students traveled to Bisho for rallies to celebrate the overthrow of President Sebe. Fortunately, no damage to churches was reported in the aftermath of the March coup.

The next morning, Gene needed to deposit money into our checking account, so I accompanied him. I also needed to get my glasses adjusted, and while we were in that particular shopping center, we had coffee at a lovely little shop. As we sat drinking our coffee, I thought of Nero who played the fiddle while Rome burned. Here I drank coffee while the people I had come to help were frightened, and I couldn't visit them. Rain fell during our month-long confinement in East London, and we hoped it would calm the people down in the Ciskei.

But it would be three years that we would feel the drumbeat of unrest. Each person had to pay R45,00 (about $25) to the Ciskei government each month, and the people eventually rebelled against it. They preferred to be in South Africa rather than under Brigadier General Oupa.

Our hearts broke for the people of the Ciskei. How they needed to know that Jesus saw them and had compassion for them, and so did we. Truly, they were like sheep without a shepherd, weary and worn out. How different that March weekend would have been if each person had known Jesus as Savior and Lord. We longed for the day when we could share Jesus' love with them again.

Chapter Eleven

JESUS FILM

He said to them, "Go into all the world and preach the good news to all creation. Whoever believes and is baptized will be saved, but whoever does not believe will be condemned."
Mark 16:15-16

On Saturday, April 7, 1990, Gene and Bob Morris went to the township of Zwelitsha to show *The Jesus Film*. After counting 170 people, Gene stopped counting. Since the pastor had the people raise their hands if they wanted to become a follower of Jesus, Gene didn't know how many decisions had been made.

The next day, I went with Gene to show the film at Mdantsane, and twenty-eight adults came forward to receive Christ as Savior. At first, we thought the appeal had been for rededications, but the pastor assured us that those people came professing Jesus for the first time. When God moved in a dramatic way, sometimes we minimized it. The pastors also told us there were many unsaved people in their churches. Evidently, this was proof since people were visibly touched by this movie.

A month earlier, every shop in Mdantsane had been burned. But as we entered, the town appeared peaceful and calm. The pastor asked me to organize a sewing class for the ladies. Although I was thrilled with the invitation, I groaned inwardly since I already had two weekly sewing classes and sometimes a third. I thought perhaps the pastor was asking for help with discipleship and not necessarily for a sewing class. So I planned to start a MasterLife Class on Saturdays for the ladies.

After we arrived home from Mdantsane, we parked our personal car in the garage since it held the TV and VCR. Gene would show the film on Wednesday night in Bisho where David Montsonga, the pastor, was leading a tent revival. From the revival outreach, they hoped to start a church.

The following Thursday night, Gene showed the film in Dimbasa, a town an hour and a half from East London. Around three hundred people squeezed into the jam-packed crusade tent. At the conclusion, an invitation was given. About sixty children and thirty-one adults made commitments to Christ. These converts were counseled, given portions of the Gospels, and offered Bibles.

It was a thrilling evening though rain poured during the film. Since we were experiencing the worst drought in fifty years, no one complained about the deluge. With grateful hearts, Gene and I were delighted to be a part of God's work in this corner of the world.

Later, in just one showing of *The Jesus Film* in Mashologu Baptist Church, sixty-six individuals made commitments to Christ. Again, Gene and I were happy to witness God at work. The film served as a beacon of light and hope to the township. We praised the Lord for the presence of the Baptist church there, and for the unique way *The Jesus Film* "preached" "the good news to all creation."

Chapter Twelve

BURNED SHACKS

My comfort in my suffering is this:
Your promise preserves my life.
Psalm 119:50

The Blacks of South Africa dealt with so many crises, I wondered how they survived.

One morning, I read in the daily newspaper that a fire broke out in Duncan Village near the street that sounded like the one we traveled on to reach Mashologu Church. Straightaway, Gene contacted Peter, the pastor, who reported that the fire was in front of the church, and he was afraid the church would burn, too.

Allegedly, the fire had started in a shack inhabited by a woman whose relatives had provided her living quarters. Later, the woman said she felt unsafe and planned to move elsewhere since angry shack dwellers wanted to attack her.

Sixty shacks had burned, leaving more than 500 people homeless. For the rest of Sunday night, they had stayed on the church grounds and had demanded storage of their personal belongings inside of Mashologu Church. Before any item could be stored, volunteers made an itemized list of each family's personal belongings. In the aftermath of the fire, the residents stayed at the new Gompo town hall, a large building. Later in the week, they would come at different times to get their belongings, but wouldn't have access unless someone was present with the record book.

As we drove past the burned area, Gene and I were saddened to see dejected people surveying the blackened remains of their shacks. Half-burned clothing, smoldering mattresses, and buckled bed frames littered the area. Women and children searched through the charred ruins for any possessions that might have escaped the fire. Men raked and cleared the ground. During our visit, the town engineer came from East London and told us that Section C of Gompo Town was in worse condition than the area that had burned. We talked with several victims.

Mrs. Butho, a resident, stated that she had lost everything, including clothes, reference books, and school certificates. Children lost their school uniforms and books. Some people who had been away for the Easter weekend returned to learn they had lost everything.

Mrs. Ndaba, another resident, said that on Sunday night she and her husband heard people screaming about the fire.

She barely had time to snatch her eight-month-old baby boy from his bed and flee ahead of the flames. The fire took hold so quickly that she wasn't able to save any of her belongings.

Mr. Genene began rebuilding immediately because he found it difficult to stay in the town hall with so many people.

After talking with these fire victims, we went inside the church. The crèche, normally by the front platform, had been moved because of the large volume of stored items. Several women swept the floor, causing clouds of dust to hang in the air. Oscarina mentioned that the smoky smell of the stored items had seeped into their living area.

Gene and I then traveled to the town hall where the now homeless people were staying. After we parked in front of the building, several small boys met us and said in Xhosa, "We know this car because they visit the minister." Their statement meant that our car was marked by the people. It was also an important designation since it wasn't safe for unfamiliar White people to enter the village. Some outsiders were looked upon as "informers" or as individuals planning to stir up the Blacks, which did happen on occasion.

Once inside the town hall, we met a Xhosa man who had come to interpret for the people. On one side of the building, several ladies sat around a rectangular table. All were eating snacks from one bowl that sat in the middle of the table.

One lady shared that she was nine months pregnant and her legs and feet were swollen.

Another man showed us samp and beans, food that had been donated. Samp, a corn product, was something like ground grits. In that same area, a couple of women prepared food on two small kerosene burners for the group.

We learned the greatest needs were blankets and baby food. The next day Gene would return to the town hall with another pastor to deliver 133 blankets that he had gathered.

On our way back to the church, we met Harriet Congiza, driving her van on one of the streets. She usually interpreted for me each Wednesday. She planned to return in a little while for Bible study, but there would be no sewing class.

While we waited, Oscarina invited us to the vestry where Peter and she lived at the back of the church with their children. During that time, Gene went and took pictures of the fire rubble.

Since Harriet didn't come back, we decided to leave around 1:30 p.m. We walked through the church and to the front steps. Beside our car we saw several people gathered. Someone said, "A man has put handcuffs on the underside of the car." When the man was asked why he did it, he simply replied, "This car is not to move."

We learned that the man was mentally challenged. Thankfully, he did not connect the handcuffs to any vital moving part. Gene tried to get them loose, but they wouldn't budge.

When we returned home, Gene used various tools, but to no avail. "It will take a hacksaw to get the handcuffs off," he said. And we didn't have one. The handcuffs stayed on.

That afternoon, a worker in the Transkei called Gene. He'd had an accident in East London, but his information was garbled. We called James Westmoreland, our supervisor in Johannesburg, to ask if we could loan our mission car to the worker. We would be in the States during May, and the mission car would sit in our garage the entire time. James saw no problem with the arrangement if we were happy with the decision.

Since traveling is the most dangerous thing we did, Gene discovered that the worker lost control of his vehicle when he swerved to avoid hitting some cows. The truck flipped, came to rest on its side, and then settled back on the front wheels. The worker could easily have been killed. We tried to get him to spend the night, but he wanted to continue home. When he returned our mission car, the handcuffs had been removed.

On April 23, 1990, I wrote the following to Mrs. Morgan, my high school English teacher:

Tonight, Gene is holding a Bible study for a pastor in Gompo Township because the pastor had a mastoidectomy last week. I really don't like for Gene to go into the township at night. There is no electricity in this part of the township. He went in our personal car, and our car is not known by the people as we normally go in the mission car. Our mission car is on loan to a fellow colleague who totaled his one last Friday near East London.

Two hours later, I was relieved when Gene returned safely.

While we worked in South Africa, we knew we could lose our lives or come to harm on any given day. It was not a safe place to live. We faced danger just like the nationals, but each morning became a new opportunity to trust the Lord. And what a comfort He was.

Our home at 18 Mayflower Terrace in Beacon Bay, South Africa and our station wagon, both provided by the International Mission Board.

Gene helps distribute grain from local individuals and charities for the Gazankulu refugees that were denied refugee status.

A gentleman learning to make candles at Ft. Beaufort. Gene taught this skill in the early days of our first term since people didn't have electricity in the villages.

The back area of Mashologu Baptist Church where Tanya taught a kindergarten class. I taught sewing and Bible classes in the front area.

The Mashologu sewing and Bible class

The sewing class at Chalumna Baptist Church displaying their work

At the Kiekammoahoek Baptist Church, Angelina Lata, the pastor's wife, learns to operate a sewing machine.

Gene teaches a training workshop for Sunday School teachers.

Teaching Umfundisi Stanford Mcitikali how to read Xhosa

The English and Xhosa classes at Ndevana Baptist Church.
Winnie Mcitikali, the pastor's wife, sits in the center.

The Tshabo Baptist Women's Department

One of Gene's Continuing Witnessing Training classes

Gene gives Daniel Mburwana his certificate for Continuing Witnessing Training.

Johannes and Angelina Lata, the pastoral couple at Keiskammahoek Baptist Church

My youth class at Dongwe Baptist Church

The Bubele Baptist Church congregation walking to the river for baptisms

Gene and Simon Dayi lead a marriage enrichment seminar at the Mdantsane Baptist Church.

Gene pictured with Ezra Dingiso, third from left, and other men working on a Certificate of Ministry at the Cape Town Baptist College (now Cape Town Baptist Seminary.)

Giving my induction message as the president of the
South African Baptist Women's Department (SABWD),
Fish Hoek Baptist Church.

Baptist Women meet in the Mashologu Baptist Church.

Women attending the Eastern Baptist Women's Department Rally in Idutywa Community Center

Oscarina Mabena and I at the SABWD
Ladies Seminar, Aventura

Jill Briscoe, left, looks on as Carol Crutchley leads the
music at the SABWD Ladies Seminar, Aventura.

Officers of the SABWD, Aventura

Ladies stand in queue for lunch at the SABWD Ladies Seminar, Aventura.

Ladies view evangelistic tracts at SABWD Ladies Seminar, Aventura.

Gene attends the graduation at Cape Town Baptist College (now Cape Town Baptist Seminary.)

Gene and I attend the Celebration of Emeriti, sponsored by the International Mission Board for retired missionaries.

Chapter Thirteen

ILLNESS IN THE MANSE

*He heals the broken-hearted and binds
up their wounds.
Psalm 147:3*

"We've been waiting fourteen months to settle this estate," my sister Maretta said to me. I sat with my brothers, Carey and Percy Thompson, in the lawyer's office. Mother had been dead for over a year, and I had not been able to come sooner to settle my parents' estate.

Later, as we sat around the dining room table at Percy's home, we faced many decisions. My father, a farmer, had owned a great deal of machinery and land. During the hours we worked, my abdomen rolled and rolled. I felt miserable.

Gene and I had looked forward to this May trip and had planned a full schedule. Our first stop was Alabama to settle the estate. Then it was on to Texas for our son Tim's college graduation in Abilene and later to Galveston, for our son-in-law's graduation from medical school. Afterwards, we traveled to New Mexico to meet our new grandson, Caleb, who was already eleven months old.

Upon our return to East London in June, Gene and I continued speaking, teaching, and visiting. I pushed myself to keep ministering like I did before we made our whirlwind trip. I led Bible studies, but after a short while, I found it difficult to keep going or even to breathe. Fatigue engulfed me. As much as I tried, I couldn't continue.

Finally, I visited Dr. Schnell, my family doctor. After sharing some things with him about myself, I ended by saying, "I need help."

He answered compassionately, "Yes, you do." He helped me get an appointment with Dr. John Woods, a psychiatrist.

When I visited Dr. Woods, he recommended that I see him once a month or check into Jenwer Convalescent Home, a treatment center for depression.

After talking with Gene, we agreed I should go to Jenwer. But I worried that my treatment would jeopardize our prospects for continuing missionary work in South Africa. Gene and I only had eighteen months left before we went back to the United States for our stateside assignment, formerly known as furlough. I wanted to make the best use of my remaining time in the country. My schedule stayed as full as

Gene's, and since we owned a personal car, we hoped to accomplish more. There was such a great need, and we loved being with the people.

"What will this do to our chance of returning to South Africa at the end of our stateside assignment?" I asked Gene.

"We have to take care of you first," Gene said in a soft voice. "If this keeps us from coming back, there will be something else for us to do."

While I waited to enter Jenwer, Gene and I attended the annual general meeting for our workers that would last a week. Only Gene knew of my plans to seek treatment at Jenwer. I felt terrible. I had come to South Africa to help, but now I was the one who needed it.

On July 23, a cold winter morning, Gene drove me to Jenwer. Afterwards, he left to attend a retreat for pastors at Morgan's Bay, a lovely place near the Indian Ocean, and an hour and a half from East London.

The office staff directed me to a room that I would share with three other ladies. My bed was by the door where each person passed as they came into the room. The building wasn't heated. That morning, I was the first person to see Dr. Woods, which helped alleviate some of my feelings about whether I could see this venture through.

Each day began with exercises followed by "climate time," a method used for conveying how we felt. A sheet contained different faces with emotional expressions. I had to pick the face that described how I felt. I picked the scared face. Each person talked about how they were feeling and marked it on the chart.

Breakfast followed and then an hour of free time. Afterwards, we had group time, teatime, relaxation therapy, and lunch time followed by more free time until 2:00 p.m. The afternoon included another group time, teatime, and relaxation therapy. The rest of the day was free although we had assignments and homework.

I felt so embarrassed to be admitted to this facility. I didn't want anyone in East London to discover me there, so whenever visiting hours came, I hid. After the third day, I wanted to go home, but since Gene was away at the pastors' retreat, I had no transportation. Of course, I entertained jealous feelings, envisioning the great time he was having at Morgan's Bay while I was in a treatment center. I didn't know if I had enough money to get a taxi ride home, but I told the nursing sister I wanted to leave.

Later at visitation time, I was in the common room and heard someone say, "Hello, Ellamae."

I saw Maurine Knudson, a friend, who had come to visit a patient. I greeted her and went over to visit with her for a while. As she prepared to leave, she responded kindly, "You are in the right place at the right time." I was happy to hear her words of encouragement and hoped other friends thought the same.

When I saw Dr. Woods that night, he asked why I didn't tell him that I wanted to leave. I told him I got sidetracked in our session the night before. He then explained to me what I was really saying: 1) I didn't want to open up and share myself 2) I didn't want to share the facilitator of the group, and 3) if I couldn't make at Jenwer, I couldn't make it anywhere since Jenwer was a microcosm of my normal world.

I remembered that in each place Gene and I had lived, I always felt like an outsider. But at Jenwer I was at a crossroads. I told myself, "Ellamae, it's now or never to deal with this matter of feeling like an outsider."

With that knowledge, I pressed forward in the program and gave it all I had. I learned from one of the nurses that my psychiatrist was quite impressed with me for not leaving and seeing it through. In the days that followed, I received different assignments to complete. One was to list my weaknesses on the left side of a sheet of paper and on the right, to list my strengths. Another assignment was to graph the main events of my life. I highlighted the death of my brother Everett.

As soon as Friday came, Dr. Woods said, "I'm going to check you out for the weekend, but I want you to return on Sunday night for the following week."

To complicate our schedule, Gene expected Carroll Shaw, a colleague, to arrive at the airport at noon. Gene would also need to help him the next day in a seminar. Since he couldn't get a flight on Saturday, he came a day early.

I told Gene not to bring Carroll when he picked me up at Jenwer. But I was eager to see Gene. We had tea together, shopped for groceries, and picked up boxes of Continuing Witnessing Training materials (CWT) at the post office.

When we entered our driveway, Carroll walked out the front door and said, "Welcome. I've been your host and secretary all afternoon." I think he caught a glimpse of our lives since he had answered our phone and doorbell numerous times.

Later that night, I went to the car to get my suitcase. Instead of taking it to the front door, I took it to the gate leading to the backyard and lowered it over the gate. I then returned back through the front door and out the back door to retrieve my suitcase. Later in our bedroom, Gene asked, "When did you get your suitcase in?" I had to admit my duplicity.

Before Gene took me back to Jenwer on Sunday night, I shared with Jeanie Hounsell, my pastor's wife, and Shirley Du Plessis, a close friend, about my stay in the facility, and that I was returning for another week.

Shirley said, "I'm so sorry I haven't come to see you since you've come back from America." I understood her to say that my situation might not have happened if she had visited me.

"It's all right, Shirley. It wouldn't have made any difference."

My struggles went much deeper.

On Monday afternoon, though, Shirley came to visit me. I was delighted to see her. She worked as a nurse in Dr. Schnell's office and informed him that I was in Jenwer. He had scheduled a visit with me on Tuesday. When he walked in, he held out his hand and said, "May I have this dance with you?"

I just fell into his arms. He sat down on my bed with me, and we chatted. I showed him the letter I had written to Joan, my friend from Aztec, who had multiple sclerosis. I never knew until our May trip to the United States that she had overdosed a year and a half earlier. I was devastated. I told Dr. Schnell that I had let Gene read my letter during the weekend and his response was, "I didn't realize she meant so much to you."

As we sat there together, Dr. Schnell told me he had experienced the same feelings I had described in my letter to Joan when he had lost a friend to suicide.

Later, during the group therapy sessions, the counselor encouraged me to write another letter, this time to Everett, the brother I lost when I was a teenager.

On Thursday morning, August 2, after we had eaten breakfast, a patient read the headlines of the *Daily Dispatch*, "Saddam Hussein, the leader of Iraq, has invaded Kuwait." Listening to the ghastly news seemed to chill the spirits of the patients, including mine. I remembered my son Tim, a member of the National Guard, and wondered how this would impact his future.

After Tim had graduated from college in May, he traveled to Virginia because Jane, his new friend, would be returning there at the end of her term assignment with our company. They planned to continue their relationship. Tim had found a job at the naval base in Dahlgren, Virginia. I wondered if his unit would be called up for active duty in the weeks to come.

On August 10, 1990, I wrote the following to Tim: *Settling the estate was a trying time for me although it was a peaceful settlement. I couldn't forget the brother I lost in drowning should have been there. I kept hearing the phrase a fourth when it should have been a fifth for each of us.*

Hearing of Joan's death was the final straw. I knew I was her closest friend. When we moved to Africa, I never wrote or called her at any time. I felt responsible to a degree in her death.

I couldn't help but remember a couple of months after we moved to Aztec in January, 1975. Joan had parked her green car in front of our house. After sitting on the sofa, she said, "I think I have multiple sclerosis."

"Joan, go to the doctor first before you come to believe this diagnosis. What makes you think you have multiple sclerosis?"

"I can't walk properly. I start out in one direction and end up going in another one."

At her doctor's request, she entered the hospital for a series of tests. Later, I went to visit her in the hospital. After we greeted each other, she told me the sad news. "Ellamae, my doctor said I had diagnosed my own case." Within a year, she was confined to a wheelchair.

During the thirteen years we lived in Aztec, I stayed in close contact with Joan and her family. I loved going to her home. One joke we shared was this: "Joan, when we get to heaven, I'm going to have a running race with you, and I'm going to win."

"Oh, you just think so. Well, watch me."

Sometimes I would take Joan to physical therapy. For a while, she was able to swing herself from the wheelchair onto the sofa. But gradually her muscles declined to where she could not manage this. One time when I helped her, I almost dropped her. From then on, when I couldn't get her to go anywhere with me, I would tease and say, "You won't go with me to the restaurant because you're afraid that I might drop you."

"Now, Ellamae, you know that's not so."

When I went to tell her goodbye before leaving Aztec for ILC, she was uncommunicative, and I wasn't able to engage her in conversation. If there was another human being who knew me and knew how I thought, it was Joan.

Joan overdosed and when she was found, it was too late to save her. After fourteen years of living in an imprisoned body, this beautiful Christian lady had had enough. I couldn't help but wonder, had I continued to live in Aztec and to maintain close contact, would this tragedy have occurred? Or would Joan have been strong enough psychologically to forge ahead, given her restrictions?

There was no funeral. Her body was cremated. The community in Aztec didn't know how or why she died since she'd been sick for years.

Ironically, as bad things continued to happen in South Africa, writing about the death of my brother caused something healthy to happen in me. Ever since we had come to the country, I attended the ladies' ministry in my church. About six weeks after my Jenwer stay, I attended a ladies' meeting. The leader had placed chairs in a circle with a pillow in front of each chair. She explained that our chair was our altar.

Each lady knelt in prayer on her pillow, faced her altar, and prayed. Praying audibly, the leader shared how her four sons had gone off to war, and each one had returned home. Two of them had been wounded, but healed without any permanent disability.

Another lady recounted how a friend of hers had a nineteen-year-old daughter with leukemia, and the daughter cried out to her parents, "Help me. I'm dying."

As I prayed silently, after a few minutes, I began to see my dear brother, lying in a coffin in the living room of my childhood home. I tried to be quiet, but I started to weep.

Jeanie, my pastor's wife, came over to me while the prayer meeting continued and said, "Let go. It's all right to cry."

It's strange how words can leave imprints on our souls. Previously spoken words had locked me in grief at the time of Everett's death. For the first time, I had been given permission to cry for the brother with whom I grew up. That day became Everett's funeral for me, and he had been dead for thirty-six years.

However, those tears were not the only ones that fell. More came in the following weeks, but I believe I finally completed the grief process for my beloved brother.

After Jenwer, Dr. Woods wanted me to take a holiday for a month because going through therapy is like going through physical surgery. I needed time to continue healing and to recover my strength, although I hesitated to take a month off from our ministries. We had scheduled out-of-town guests, a family camp, and two weeks of back-to-back Continuing Witnessing Training.

In a generic letter to my children on September 10, 1990, I wrote, *I really wish I could write each of you an individual letter now and tell you about all the good times we're having in our ministries. Of course, it goes without our saying that we are having our rough moments as the country seems to grow in violence. We continue to pray the Prince of Peace will bring peace to our troubled land.*

My experience at Jenwer caused a peaceful change in me. For the first time in my life, I felt abundantly free of the emotional baggage that had weighed me down. I learned that freedom comes from reliving trauma with a trusted counselor in a safe environment. Negative emotions are stripped away when we talk honestly about what we've experienced. As the Lord's "work in progress," resolving my mental health issues made me more the person God wanted me to be. I felt free, like I was walking on a cloud.

Chapter Fourteen

REAPING IN THE HARVEST

Then He (Jesus) said to his disciples, "The harvest is plentiful, but the workers are few. Ask the Lord of the harvest, therefore, to send out workers into his harvest field."
Matthew 9:37-38

I grew up on a farm in southern Alabama. Each spring, my father would climb on a tractor and head off to prepare the fields for planting. My brothers would help with the various farming tasks. My job was to plant a vegetable garden and watch and weed it until harvest time. Afterwards came canning and freezing the produce.

Throughout the growing season, my father would check the progress of the plants. I'll always remember carrying him a water jug, wrapped in newspaper to keep the water cold. From sunup until sundown, he worked tirelessly until the day came to "reap the fruit of his labor." It was a time of great satisfaction.

Farming requires long hours and hard work. Harvesting crops doesn't just happen. Farmers must prepare the soil before planting seeds. The fields must then be tended and watered for growth to occur. Only when these steps are complete will the farmer see a harvest. As a missionary in South Africa, I was now "farming," but in a different sense. I was laboring for a "spiritual harvest."

During the winter of 1990, Gene and I traveled to the Indian Church in Chatsworth. We helped with a Continuing Witnessing Training (CWT) program that lasted three days. The course taught Christians how to share their faith more effectively. During the daytime training, an "equipper" would work with two individuals and teach them to present the gospel. In addition, the two individuals would learn spiritual truths. During the evening hours, the equipper and the two trainees would go out together to homes in the community to "plant the seeds of the gospel." Ordinarily, a church conducted this program for thirteen weeks.

At Chatsworth, I became an equipper to Aneil and Edwin, two Indian pastors. On the first night as we went out, I shared the gospel presentation with an Indian man. He stood in the corner of his living room the entire time. Afterwards, I asked him, "Is there any reason why you would not be willing to receive eternal life?"

The man answered cautiously, "I have never heard anything like this before, and I will have to do some more learning about this God you speak of."

To keep the door open for further witness, I didn't push. However, I couldn't forget the way the man listened with rapt attention and looked directly at me the whole time.

In the dining room nearby, the man's mother had sat quietly, listening to our conversation. Afterwards, the man's wife served us tea. When we finished our tea, the man introduced us to his tenants, who lived in the flat (apartment) in his back garden (yard). They were Christians. Perhaps they would continue to "water the seeds of the gospel" that we had planted.

My time with this Indian man also reminded me of Esther Abraham, an Indian missionary, who had her own style of witnessing. I had met Esther two years earlier at the weeklong camp at Barachel. This beautiful lady would ask her Hindu friends, "Does your god answer you when you pray?" The answer was always no. She would then respond, "My God does!" Her enthusiastic reply would spark interest. Sometimes, "farmers" use different techniques to harvest. Esther certainly did.

On the second night of the training course, Edwin presented the gospel. On the final night, no one appeared to be home. I had worn heeled boots, even though the Durbin winter was mild, and I was getting tired. I wondered what we should do. I prayed silently. *Lord, we're out here to tell these people about You. We aren't finding anyone at home. Where do You want us to go at this moment?*

We spotted a flat in the dimly lit street and walked toward it. Lights from a hallway and television streamed through a window. A young man sat in front of the television. Before we entered the yard, Aneil whistled to alert any dog that might be present. (Whistling was always a good idea since there were many dogs in South Africa.)

When Aneil knocked, the young man opened the door and a German shepherd slipped out. Thankfully, the dog greeted us in a friendly manner. Claude, the young man, invited us in.

After we sat down, we learned Claude was in "matric," equivalent to twelfth grade in the United States. We chatted for a while before Aneil began to share the gospel presentation. He asked Claude, "Do you know for certain that you have eternal life and that you will go to heaven when you die?"

Claude wasn't sure. Aneil responded that God wanted him to be sure. He then read

1 John 5:13-15: "I write these things to you who believe in the name of the Son of God so that you may know that you have eternal life. This is the confidence we have in approaching God: that if we ask anything according to His will, He hears us. And if we know that he hears us—whatever we ask—we know that we have what we asked of him."

Claude seemed puzzled. He asked, "How did you happen to come to my house tonight?" He then told us he had attempted suicide the week before by overdosing on pills. He remembered waking up in a hospital. I wondered if God had spared Claude's life, perhaps for this very moment.

Aneil continued, "We are out to share that God loves us. He sent His Son to die for our sins."

"But how do I know I'll have eternal life when I die?"

"We're all sinners by nature," Aneil answered. "We can't save ourselves. God provided forgiveness for our sins through Jesus. When we come to Jesus, we receive salvation and eternal life. Jesus is the God/man who died on the cross for our sins. He was resurrected from the dead three days later. He died that we might have abundant life now and eternal life upon death. It's a free gift."

Happily, Claude wanted to know how to have eternal life.

"Repent of your sins," Claude answered, "which is like a car making a U-turn. Then, place your faith in Jesus, which is like taking a trip on an airplane. But you must board the plane to take the trip."

We were thrilled when Claude prayed and asked Jesus to be his Savior and Lord.

Aneil went on to explain the next steps: letting Jesus take control of his life and identifying with Jesus by confessing Him publicly through baptism.

Before we left, I hugged Claude and said, "I'm so glad you were not successful at taking your life. A year ago, a close friend of mine committed suicide. It was heart-wrenching. God saved you for a purpose. No matter what problems we have, they are only temporary. Suicide is a drastic step to take for a temporary problem. I will be praying for you."

As we returned to the church to report on our visit, I felt like I was walking on air. God, the Great Farmer of all human hearts, had used our labors to reap a sweet harvest in Claude's life. It was so exciting to be a part of bringing this young man to the Lord. Our time with Claude became the highlight of my few days in Chatsworth.

On our flight back to East London, I sat in the middle seat next to an Afrikaans man who occupied the window seat. Gene sat in the aisle seat. The Afrikaans man was attending his nephew's wedding, whose parents were deceased. When he discovered we were American expatriates, he asked why we'd come to Durban.

"We were helping our workers in a witnessing seminar," I explained. I also showed him the eternal life booklet we had used while there, and then I handed it to him.

"May I keep this?" he asked.

"Of course!"

During the flight, I noticed the man was reading the booklet. When he'd finished, I asked, "Do you understand what you have been reading?"

Immediately, he answered, "Yes, I am a Christian, and I want to share this booklet with my twin brother who lives in East London."

In East London, we continued to share the Continuing Witnessing Training program with area churches. Many people became excited "laborers" and used the gospel presentation to introduce their friends and neighbors to Jesus. As a result of this activity, churches continued to thrive and grow in the surrounding villages and towns.

Just like a physical harvest, a "spiritual harvest" doesn't just happen. The Lord of the harvest prepares the soil of the human heart. He sends laborers to plant, water and tend the seeds of the gospel. And in His timing and in His way, He reaps a plentiful harvest.

CHAPTER FIFTEEN

A LETTER TO MY CHILDREN

But in your hearts set apart Christ as Lord. Always be prepared to give an answer to everyone who asks you to give the reason for the hope that you have. But do this with gentleness and respect.
1 Peter 3:15

Dear Children,   February 23, 1991

I must tell you, yesterday was quite a day. I had the Ministers Wives Fraternal meeting at our home. The weather was hot and humid, due to the recent rains. Rebecca, my helper, came and worked a great deal. Daddy was the babysitter for the little ones with Rebecca helping him. It was a pretty day. Under the spreading big tree in our backyard, I laid a comforter down. Daddy put out the card table for serving the little ones a drink and cookies to eat. There's a nice swing in the backyard, and once during the meeting, I saw Rebecca swinging little Shayla, a three-year-old of Terry and John Basson of Stirling Church, who came there to be pastor on January 1, 1991.

Before the meeting, two Xhosa men came by at different times. The first one was Wellington, the one who was saved last week. He told Rebecca that since he only worked two days, he didn't believe in God anymore. Through Rebecca I told him, you have to wait on God sometimes for His answer. Sometimes He doesn't always answer prayers like we want.

I had Rebecca fix two slices of bread sandwiched together with peanut butter, and I told him I had a meeting and he must "Hamba Kakuhle," meaning "go well." In a few minutes, I heard someone else at the door. It was a young chap. After listening to his problem, we gave him bread, a Bible, and a Xhosa tract of the Gospel since he could read and sent him on his way. In a few minutes, he was back saying he wanted to learn about God, that he had never heard about Him. Rebecca answered the door and said, "There is a meeting here this morning. If you come back in a couple of hours, the 'inkosikazi' (lady) will tell you."

At 1:00 p.m., he "pitched" up as they say here, and I told him we were getting ready to eat, and I'd be with him in 30 minutes. At 1:30 p.m., I went to look for him and found him asleep under the palm tree on the grass by our street in front of our house. A strong scent penetrated the air as he came in and sat with Rebecca on the sofa. I sat on our love seat. To myself I'm thinking, he wants to know about God. If he wants to know about God, I am going to start with Genesis and tell him the thread of the story, leading up to the birth of Jesus, His teaching years, death, burial, and resurrection.

After giving him this information, I went into the presentation of the gospel. A new name was written in the Lamb's Book of Life and angels rejoiced again over a new one saved. I was impressed with this young man. After completing Standard 2 (Grade 4 in the States), he had to go to work because his father died. He had an older brother and sister. His brother died from being stabbed in Johannesburg. He lives with his sister on a farm near the Floradale Nursery. Sharing with him took an hour and a half. I couldn't help but wonder if he may very well be the answer to our prayers for God to call Xhosa men into the ministry. His name is Konose, and he is twenty years old.

Then that night, we went to a promotional dinner at Gonubie. At this meeting, I had to give a few sentences on "We Care Enough to Teach" when the ladies gave their part as Baptist Women.

Rebecca is here, and I just heard Daddy ask about breakfast. I told him I wanted to finish this letter. I want French toast and chocolate syrup for breakfast. It isn't a Saturday unless we have it. (Well, I have just returned from eating breakfast and having family devotions with your father. I am thinking about having Rebecca join us for the family devotions.)

I need to prepare today for MasterLife at Mdantsane in Zone 2 where I teach the ladies. These ladies read, understand, and write English. The course is written in English. I just called the pastor to ask if Rebecca could come to this class, and he is quite happy for her to do so. When I shared the news with Rebecca, she was so happy. We will leave at 3:00 p.m. and arrive at the church by 3:30 p.m. The course I teach is for two hours and the Theological Education Course Daddy teaches is also for two hours. I am really excited about teaching this course. I taught MasterLife in our church in Aztec and found it to be one of the best discipleship tools I ever used. God used MasterLife in a miraculous way to get me to give up teaching and to be willing to go where He wanted me to go. I never dreamed He would take me to another country.

All I need to do for Kimberly's afghan is to fringe it and I will have it in the mail to her. I still have a dress that needs finishing. I need to hem the sleeves and sew them into the dress. That is all I need to do, and it will be finished. Maybe I'll be able to do that tonight. After I finish this letter, I need to have my quiet time and then my study review for my lesson this afternoon. I will also be showing Rebecca how to prepare lasagna. I need to shampoo my hair and curl it as I ran in the rain this morning.

Oops! My space is gone again. I love you.

CHAPTER SIXTEEN

STATESIDE ASSIGNMENT

*Jesus...said, "Go home to your own people and
tell them how much the Lord has done for you,
and how he has had mercy on you."*
Mark 5:19

1992

After our furniture was packed up, stored, and our house on Mayflower Terrace rented, we looked forward to our stateside assignment. The old name for the stateside assignment was "furlough"—a time to present our missionary work at World Mission Conferences, camps, and churches. It was also a time to rest and relax with family and friends and prepare to return to our mission field with needed ministry supplies. Further, we planned to enroll in a marriage enrichment seminar that would enable us to lead seminars in South Africa when we returned. We'd had many requests for this kind of ministry. At that time, fifty percent of South African marriages suffered breakdowns.

However, since we would fly from South Africa to Switzerland, we planned a trip through Europe. In my journal, dated April 13, 1992, I wrote: *At the Mestre station in Milan, Italy, waiting for the train to take us to the Santa Lucia station, we saw a pigeon with a missing foot. Standing beside the platform, we watched it walking on the train track. It managed with a little more time and concentration to cross the track. Its leg with the missing foot slipped a couple of times, but it plodded on, never considering stopping in its struggle.*

My mind took me back to that time when I saw the seagull with a missing foot and how the Lord spoke to me. He said, "You feel like the seagull did living here in South Africa. But as the seagull has managed with its handicap in its environment, so you will make it living here in South Africa." Today I felt the power of those fulfilled words.

After we arrived in the USA, the first order of business was to find a car. Some months before, we had reserved a missionary residence in Memphis, TN. I thought it strange that the house did not have a fence around it nor did it have a garage. We had been used to living behind burglar bars and security gates in South Africa.

While our daughter and her family visited us, someone tried to steal her car. If the neighbor had not seen them and warned us, the thief would have succeeded. We still didn't have a car, but Gene found a 1984 Buick in a car lot. It felt like driving a tank compared to our small mission car. In South Africa, we had to be extra careful and stay in the left lane when driving. Once, I almost got into the wrong lane. If I had not stopped at a traffic light, I would have turned left into the right lane. When I stopped, I realized what I was about to do. Back in the United States, I had to reverse that order and be watchful to remain in the right lane. Likewise, when I crossed the street in South Africa, I looked left then right. Again, I had to reverse the process in the United States.

During mission weekends, world mission conferences, and camps, leaders requested women missionary speakers. I often spoke during the Sunday morning church services. At first, I found it overwhelming because of the advanced media technology.

In March, Yates Baptist Association had invited Gene and me to participate in their World Mission Conference (WMC). Earlier, we had made plane reservations for the trip. On the plane from Nashville to Durham, North Carolina, we met James Wright, a missionary of the North American Mission Board who would also be involved in the WMC. After we arrived on Saturday afternoon, we attended a church dinner for the guest missionaries and a meeting afterwards. At the meeting, I received a great amount of information about my speaking itinerary—dates, travel details, places where I would speak. I even needed to specify what I would like to eat. I looked forward to my first engagement at Temple Baptist Church. I would speak during the morning service.

The next day, I gathered my supplies. The church van arrived at the Holiday Inn to take me to Temple Baptist Church. In the Adult III Sunday school assembly, I met Russell Baldwin who welcomed me with a hug. I read one of my letters to my children during the assembly. Afterwards, I went to speak to the children's assembly. I showed pictures and a map of Africa on a display board. I described each picture that illustrated a mission activity. I also enjoyed telling them about each of my curios.

The time came for the worship service. During the children's sermon, I found myself holding a microphone and my Bible while I used a world globe to tell how Christians are commanded to go into all the world and share the gospel (Matthew 28:19-20).

Afterwards, I addressed the congregation, sharing how the Lord had used us while we were in South Africa. At the conclusion of the service, the pastor invited me to stand with him at the front door to greet the people as they left. I heard many lovely words about the service and our work.

About 4:45 p.m., Andy Bergquist and his young son Garrett met me at the hotel to take me to his house for a South African dinner. The Girls' Auxiliary and their leader were also there. Out on the patio, we ate bobotie and rice, a yogurt with cucumbers, peanut butter soup, and a crepe.

Later, I spoke at another church during the evening service. Dr. Mosely, the pastor, introduced me as the speaker and surprised me by saying he had lived in Greenville, Alabama during second and third grade. He had attended First Baptist Church. Dr. Otis Williams had been the pastor. I shared that I was one of the campers Dr. Williams had taken to Shocco Springs camp, where I had participated in the state Bible drill.

Gene and I spent many more wonderful days, speaking at World Mission Conferences, working as camp missionaries, and sharing in many different places. People showed interest and appreciation for the work we did.

We had the privilege of attending a Missions Impact Conference in Woodstock, Georgia. It was delightful to stay in the home of Don and Marge Van Meter since they had a son who was also a missionary in South Africa. While attending the Georgia conference, we met missionaries from other organizations and were inspired by their stories of what their lives and ministries were like.

During our time in the United States, I was relieved to be away from the political struggle in South Africa. However, Gene and I stayed attentive to the news coming out of the country and knew when bad events occurred. Sadly, we mourned the massacre that took place in Bisho in September.

We wanted to spend Thanksgiving with David and his family in Aztec, our former home. But a snowstorm had moved across Oklahoma, the Texas panhandle, and New Mexico. Amarillo, Texas, was paralyzed with snow. News channels reported one hundred cars had piled up.

We made good time until we arrived in Elk City, Oklahoma, but the 140 miles from Elk City to Amarillo on Interstate 40 took over four hours. The roads were iced over and treacherous. On one long stretch, traffic barely moved. We managed to bypass the congestion. Happily, on Thanksgiving Day, we arrived in Aztec for a happy dinnertime celebration.

When it came time to think about returning to South Africa, Joy expressed fear. I had misgivings also. However, I knew the Lord was leading us back. In my devotional time one morning, I read Genesis 46:1-4 where Jacob learned that Joseph was alive in Egypt. The famine in Israel was in full swing. The Lord told Jacob not to be afraid to go to Egypt. He assured Jacob that He would bring him back. Also, He told him that the hand of Joseph would close his eyes.

With these words, we believed that our faithful God would keep His promises and see us through another mission term.

Chapter Seventeen

MOTHER'S DAY 1993

*And He arose, and rebuked the wind,
and said unto the sea, "Peace, be still!"
And the wind ceased, and there was a great calm.*
Mark 4:39

While the country plunged deeper into political violence, Pauline Houlie, the pastor's wife of Parkside Baptist Church, asked me to bring the Mother's Day message. I spent much time in prayer and thought a message that spoke to the fearful hearts of the people would be appropriate.

Violent crime had escalated to new heights, and fear permeated the country. No one was safe or the "right color." The slogan of the African National Congress (ANC), the largest political entity in South Africa, was "Umkhonto we Sizwe" *(Spear of the Nation).* The armed wing of the ANC used this chant.

We continued to read of killings, fifty-seven per day on average, the highest of any year of the political movement.

Gun sales were on the rise. Five people were killed at the Highgate Hotel bar in East London. A Rhodesian (Zimbabwean) war veteran's actions prevented further loss. Following this, the ANC lifted the consumer boycott to ease tensions in our region.

On April 10, 1993, Chris Hani, the leader of the Communist party, was assassinated. On April 14, "Black Wednesday" became a day of rampant violence in Cape Town, Port Elisabeth, Pietermaritzburg, Durban, and Johannesburg. One street in Durban became a war zone.

In my journal on April 16, 1993, I wrote: *"The nation of SA mourns the death of Chris Hani…who lived near Boksburg. He had let his bodyguard off for the Easter weekend to be with his family and later was assassinated."*

Eighty-two memorial services were held for Mr. Hani. In East London, 25,000 people attended the memorial service for the slain leader. The people marched out of Duncan Village. Some came up Oxford Street, all on their way to Jan Smuts Stadium. If the rest of the country had responded like the East London crowd, the day would be remembered as a positive tribute to Chris Hani and the nation. The violence reminded us over and over again of the anger and frustration of the people, particularly the youth. They grew weary of White minority rule.

Within this atmosphere, I prepared a message of inspiration and perseverance in faith to counteract those fearful and anger-filled days. I prayed it would give hope and encouragement. The following is the message I gave:

Peace Be Still

I greet you in the name of our lovely Lord Jesus Christ, the name that is above every name. One day every knee will bow and every tongue will confess Him as Lord (Phil. 2:9-10).

I am happy to be with you ladies again and am thrilled you are still meeting and studying the Bible together.

This morning, I have chosen a Bible message to comfort our hearts and help us persevere during the darkness in our country. I hope we will take courage from it. If I were to give it a title, I would use, "Peace! Be Still!" Many of us are mothers, grandmothers, and great-grandmothers. We want to know our children will have food, shelter, clothing, and an education. We want them to live in a safe place. More than this, we want them to grow up to know and love the Lord and develop a strong faith in Him. My prayer often for my children and grandchildren is that no matter what the future holds, they will always be true to Jesus.

I have had many scary moments in my life as a Christian. One time came in 1962 when we lived at our first pastorate in Mississippi not far from Florida. Cuba, a Communist island, ninety miles from Florida, is supported by Russia (then the Soviet Union) with missiles and arms. Key American cities had been targeted for destruction by those missiles. I still remember how concerned and frightened many people were. In my arms, I held our second child, a newborn baby daughter and wondered if she would live to grow up. Never has there been a safe time for a baby to come into this world.

Today, we are concerned about what the future holds for the children growing up in South Africa. Many of our country's children do not know what it is to go to school. They don't know what a home safe from violence is. If Jesus does not come soon, I wonder what life will be like in South Africa one year from now, ten years, or even fifty years.

Last year, we spent several months in the USA. My husband and I were appalled at how crime had escalated there. Our furlough residence was located in Memphis, Tennessee, in the heart of the Old South. This region used to be a safe place to live, but now it was in a bad neighborhood. The house had a burglar alarm and security gates. Never had I lived in a house with a burglar alarm and security gates in the USA.

Our world seems caught in a collision course where we feel powerless and helpless. We stand on the brink of the chasm and watch the gulf of violence, crime, and murder widen.

For our scripture, I want us to look at a Bible story of Jesus, the One who makes a difference. He continues to change the lives and circumstances of His people. In Mark 4:35-41, we read: "That day when evening came, He said to His disciples, 'Let us go over to the other side.' Leaving the crowd behind, they took him along, just as He was, in the boat. There were also other boats with Him. A furious squall came up, and the waves broke over the boat, so that it was nearly swamped. Jesus was in the stern, sleeping on a cushion. The disciples woke Him and said to Him, 'Teacher, don't you care if we drown?' He got up, rebuked the wind and said to the waves, 'Quiet! Be still!' Then the wind died down and it was completely calm. He said to His disciples, 'Why are you so afraid? Do you have no faith?' They were terrified and asked each other, 'Who is this? Even the wind and the waves obey Him!'"

Jesus spent the day with people who lined the shore of the beautiful Galilee Lake. The number of people who followed Him was so large that He climbed into a boat to push away from the shore. On this day, He taught them the parables of the Sower, the lamp on a stand, the growing seed, and the mustard seed.

In the evening, Jesus told His disciples, "Let us go over to the other side." Afterwards, He moved to the back of the boat and went to sleep. Other boats accompanied the boat Jesus was in. While the disciples rowed the boat out into the lake, one of the storms, common to the Jordan valley, whipped up. The strong winds can trigger sheets of water as high as four and a half yards or five meters in the lake.

Something like this may have occurred while the disciples manned the boat. They felt the wind blow across the lake as they saw the dark clouds on the horizon. Hearing the thunderclaps, they saw the lightning zigzagging in the sky. As fishermen, they knew the nature of this storm and had a keen understanding of their dilemma. They were afraid. They were in danger. They struggled with the small unseaworthy boat. As they continued, they knew Jesus could help them, but He was asleep in the stern of the boat.

The disciples had been charged with the responsibility from Jesus to take the boat to the other side of the lake. Now with the boat filling with water, they faced death by drowning. In their fear they awoke Jesus and asked, "Teacher, don't you care if we drown?"

Jesus spoke to the wind and waves. In the King James Version of the Bible, He said, "Peace! Be Still!" (Mark 4:39). The Creator of the wind and the waves had spoken. Instantly, the wind ceased and the sea became calm.

After Jesus took care of the storm, He turned to His disciples and asked, "Why are you so afraid?" Is He not speaking to our hearts this morning and asking us the same question? We are His children and His creation.

In this story, I don't know what the disciples were more afraid of—the storm or the manner in which Jesus calmed the storm. The Bible tells us they were terrified, so terrified they asked each other, "Who is this? Even the wind and the waves obey Him!"

We can recognize where His power came from. "Very early in the morning, while it was still dark, Jesus got up, left the house and went off to a solitary place, where He prayed."
(Mark 1:35).

Jesus knew where His power lay and the place from where He came. Jesus knew how to stay in touch with His Father. Jesus had a time and a place to be alone with God. Being alone with His Father prepared Him to face the multitude of people with their problems. For was it not Jesus who said, "I have told you these things, so that in Me you may have peace. In this world you will have trouble. But take heart! I have overcome the world." (John 16:33)

A hurricane is a whirling storm measuring several hundred miles/kilometers. Its winds can blow 150 miles an hour or more. It is formed over the ocean in warm regions. With its fury, a hurricane can sweep into a coastal city and wreak havoc. It knocks down electrical lines, makes trees fall, blows roofs off houses, and strong houses are twisted like cardboard. Massive flooding accompanies the hurricane.

Yet, an eye is in the midst of the hurricane. This eye measures from five miles/eight kilometers to nineteen miles/thirty-three kilometers. In the eye, you will find little wind and cloudiness. Planes can enter the eye with scientists who can study the intensity of the storm. In the eye of a hurricane, one is safe.

At the edge of the eye, the fury of the hurricane begins. At sea, a hurricane is a menace to ships with its powerful winds, but in the eye of the hurricane, one is safe, traveling in an airplane.

In the midst of our hurricane in South Africa is an eye. As Christians, Jesus lives in us. John, the beloved disciple, wrote: "…greater is He that is in you, than He that is in the world."

(1 John 4:4, KJV).

We need to be quiet and meet God alone in prayer and read His Word each day. A Christian can pray anytime and anywhere. In these days, we cannot do without a special time and place to meet with God like Jesus did. It is in these times with God that we get our power and strength for each day. The struggles of our lives are overcome in communion at God's table, for there is our "Daily Bread."

In Gethsemane, in the dark hour when Jesus faced the cross, He prayed. Is it any wonder when He was called upon to die for us, He looked into heaven and beheld His father's face and said, "…not My will, but Thine, be done." (Luke 22:42, KJV) Jesus had overcome in His prayer times, talking with His Father.

Years ago, fear marched under a different name across Europe. In France there lived a dictator named Napoleon who stalked Europe with his massive army.

Citizens of Feldkirch, Austria, had spotted his soldiers in the heights of the mountains. The councilmen met, asking, "What must we do? Shall we try to defend ourselves or display the white flag of surrender?"

It was Easter, and the people had already gathered for the worship services.

The pastor rose and said, "Friends, we have been counting on our own strength, and apparently that has failed. As this is the day of our Lord's Resurrection, let us just ring the bells, have our services as usual, and leave the matter in His hands. We know only our weakness and not the power of God to defend us."

The councilmen accepted the plan and someone rang the church bells. When Napoleon's soldiers heard the church bells toll, they thought the Austrian army had arrived during the night to save the town. Before the service ended, the enemy broke camp and left.[12]

There is a saying, "Fear knocked at the door, Faith answered, and no one was there."

Throughout the Bible we have one story after another of how God protected and preserved His people in times of crises. Our names are written on the palm of His hand, and no harm will come to us without His permission.

After the service, many people expressed their appreciation for the message. One man spoke to Gene, "I came to church discouraged, and I am leaving inspired and encouraged."

With Jesus living in us, we can face our difficulties, for *He* is our peace.

---

[12] Homiletics Class of West Coast Baptist College, "The Sound of Church Bells," *Ministry127.com,*, 2024

CHAPTER EIGHTEEN

MISSION MEETING 1994

Have I not commanded you? Be strong and courageous.
Do not be terrified; do not be discouraged, for the Lord
your God will be with you wherever you go.
Joshua 1:9

Standing outside in the autumn of the March morning, Haskell and Elaine Wilson, Gene, and I talked about the dreadful incidents and disasters taking place in South Africa. We had watched the political violence for years. We wondered whether we should leave or stay in South Africa during the upcoming elections, just weeks away. Each worker in our company had to make that decision.

In this beautiful place, the trees boasted leaves in crimson, russet gold, and pale yellow. I looked around at the scenery and thought how tragic that in this lovely country with wonderful people, the political climate had plummeted so deeply. I said, "I think each group has polarized."

"I think you're right," Haskell replied. "Things look bad."

Each year, the workers of our company gathered for an annual mission meeting. In 1994, we met at The Wigwam in Rustenburg in northwest South Africa. Workers came from all over the country. Others, stationed in Lesotho, Swaziland, Botswana, and Namibia, assembled for their meetings, too.

Company business occurred each morning and afternoon. At night, we assembled for worship services. Terry Rae, the executive director of the Baptist Union, was the plenary speaker. Each night, he preached inspiring and uplifting sermons. He reported that everyone in South Africa was afraid. I knew I was afraid. I also remembered the statement, "*Everybody is the wrong color in South Africa.*" But with anger and hate growing exponentially through the years, none of those statements helped me as I weighed our situation. Nevertheless, Terry ministered to our anguished hearts and fearful minds, assuring us that God would meet us where we were.

As the meeting continued, I heard different workers talk about taking the company's equipment, even the cars, if they left before the elections. This would ensure preservation of the equipment. I thought their arguments made sense. Further, to prepare for every scenario and increasing danger, our company provided plane tickets. They also required each worker to submit an escape plan. At that point, there was still time to plan on leaving.

All too soon, the meeting ended, and we headed south for East London. As we traveled deeper into the country, we saw more evidence of violence. I will never forget the burned frame of a still-smoking tractor-trailer truck and debris beside the road. As I viewed other equally disturbing sights along our route, I hoped we would make the right decision about whether to stay or leave. Should the country go to war, we would save a great deal if we left and relocated to Zimbabwe.

When the meeting concluded, I thought maybe we *should* leave the country since we still had time. The option to go to Zimbabwe seemed attractive because the country was calmer and more peaceful than South Africa. Missionaries who had served there had many glowing things to say about the country and its people. Since I had never traveled to Zimbabwe before, I found myself wanting to go. I thought it might be a good option.

In the midst of all these thoughts and emotions, we wanted to know God's will. During our quiet time with the Lord, He revealed to us that we were to stay in South Africa, even though we knew our children wanted us to leave.

When we returned to East London, Gene wrote to the children on March 24, 1994: *We have prepaid airline tickets that are good for a year that will get us out of the country should that be necessary. Believe me, we will use them if the situation worsens to the point that we no longer feel that we can stay. Right now, our decision is to stay during the elections (some of our missionaries are evacuating during that time and we don't blame them) because we feel safe in our present setup. As you know, the security at our house has been enhanced by our company and we feel safe there. We also believe that our credibility would be damaged if we left. After all, our friends and the people with whom we work cannot leave.*

Since we were staying, we needed to stock a six-month supply of items, such as food and other necessities should the country experience civil war, and we believed it would. As the days drew closer to the election, that outcome seemed inevitable.

We felt we needed to stay with our people. But if things went bad for the country and for us, we also knew we lived in the presence of the Lord. He would be with us regardless of what happened. He told us not to be terrified or discouraged. To calm our hearts and minds, we needed to remember that we dwelt in the shelter of Almighty God. A better day was up ahead.

CHAPTER NINETEEN

PEACE AND FREEDOM AT LAST

*Many are the plans in a man's heart,
but it is the Lord's purpose that prevails.
Proverbs 19:21*

At last, the time had come for the first democratic election. The sun smiled on the day that the Colored, Asians, and Blacks had dreamed of for a long, long time. Since the previous June, the people had waited for these elections to take place.

But throughout 1993, we had read and heard about terrible tragedies. Even close friends told us about murders occurring within their neighborhoods. In Mdantsane, a couple's house was petrol-bombed. They had ties to the United Democratic Front (UDF). Both were severely burned, but fortunately, their children escaped injury, although one had to be treated for shock. The week before the election, buildings near the International Airport in Johannesburg had been bombed. However, people remained optimistic, but guarded about what they saw on television, read in the newspapers, and heard from friends and neighbors.

On April 14, 1994, Transkei, east of East London, lowered their flag for the last time. Four days later, Ciskei, the homeland to the west and north of East London, lowered their flag for the last time. When Transkei, Ciskei, and the other homelands lowered their flags, they were reincorporated into South Africa.

In a letter to my daughter, dated April 26, 1994, I wrote: *We heard over the news last night of the bombings in the Joburg area killing 21 people, twice the number of people who get killed daily in South Africa these days. Many were injured and lots of damage was done to buildings. The right wing stated they would escalate their activities in the time prior to the election and perhaps they are keeping their word. In our area, it is quiet and peaceful.*

A general peace has reigned in many hearts here since the Inkatha Freedom Party (IFP) joined the election process. We plan to vote either tomorrow or the next day. The days to vote are covering three days. People in the hospital at Frere in EL (East London) will be voting. I think I read even prisoners will get to vote. This is all a little strange to me, considering our method of election. I think people could pad the election the way it is being carried out.

On that joyful election day, Gene and I walked out on the veranda, down the steps by our palm trees, and headed for the polling station at St. Nicholas Church Hall. In our community, people from all ethnic groups walked down each street that fed into Bonza Bay Street, the main thoroughfare to the church. We joined the throng in the excitement of this monumental day when all South Africans could vote.

As we neared, we saw a line that branched out from the polling station. We knew the line would be long. Since we arrived early in the day, we hoped we wouldn't have to wait too long, but we found ourselves nearly three blocks away from the church.

While standing in line, I remembered my conversation with Ethne Buckner, a recent dinner guest. There in my kitchen, she asked, "Are you going to vote?"

"I can't vote here. I am not a citizen," I answered.

"Don't you have permanent residency here?"

"Yes. But that doesn't qualify me to vote."

"Yes, it does. They have made a loophole for people like Walter Sisulu and others who have been in exile to vote. The people who have permanent residency can also vote."

"Wow! I never thought of voting in the election. Now I can."

As we stood with the sun beaming down on us, we had fun talking to people of different ethnicities. Soon, a man came by selling cans of soda pop. Of course, we bought two since we were thirsty.

Eventually, we made it to the steps that lead into the church hall where the voting process began. Election officials occupied a long table. I received a stamp on my right hand, a pencil, and a ballot with nineteen candidates listed from each of the country's political parties. One lady motioned me to a voting station that resembled a tall corrugated box, bent in two places to form a booth. I voted for a candidate, then left the booth and handed the lady my pencil and ballot. She placed my ballot through the slit in a box where the ballots were collected.

I met up with Gene and we walked out the back door and headed home. Afterwards, we decided to see what the other polling stations looked like. At each place, we saw longer lines than the one we had stood in.

Later, we heard that an older Black lady from one of the villages had waited fourteen hours to vote. For over three hundred years the Blacks had waited to vote in their country, and we only waited an hour and a half. It didn't feel right.

But on that day, God answered many, many prayers because crime plummeted. Everywhere we traveled, people were happy and smiling. A feeling of euphoria reigned over the day. Peace and freedom had won, and the Lord's purpose had prevailed.

Chapter Twenty

A LIGHT IN THE DARKNESS

Your word is a lamp to my feet
and a light to my path.
Psalm 119:105

Around 1869, Baptist work began in Tshabo, Ciskei. About 125 years later, I had the privilege of launching a literacy ministry in this village. Umfundisi (*Minister*) Stanford Mcitakali was my first student.

I had heard about Stanford, a pastor who couldn't read. To help him prepare his sermons, his daughter read the Bible to him. Since I was a former schoolteacher, I felt a keen desire to teach this man how to read. Our co-worker asked him if he would like to learn. Initially, he said no. I was disappointed, but months later, he moved nearer to East London and changed his mind.

In August of 1994, Gene and I found our way to Tshabo, an hour's drive from East London. A week later, I traveled alone to meet Stanford for his first lesson at the church where he pastored. I dressed in layers and wore my all-weather coat since the buildings in South Africa had no central heating or cooling. The temperature remained the same, both inside and outside. I also wore a long denim skirt since Xhosa women did not wear pants.

Despite the musty smell, the sanctuary was well furnished with nice oak pews and a communion table, draped with a white cloth. A wooden railing framed the front of the platform. Steps rose on either side, and a pulpit stood in the center. I later learned the church had previously belonged to a White congregation.

I greeted the pastor, a man of short stature with ebony skin and short fuzzy black hair. He wore a navy sweater vest over his white shirt along with a tie and suit coat.

"Molo, Umfundisi (*Hello, Minister*)," I said in Xhosa.

"Molo, madam *(Good morning, madam),*" he answered.

"Kunjani, Umfundisi? *(How are you, Minister?)*"

"Philile, ewe? *(Well, and you?)*"

"Ndipilile. Enkos. (*I am well. Thank you.)*"

I think Stanford was as excited and edgy as I was. We walked toward the communion table. Before I sat down, I touched the gorgeous wooden railing and said, "It is beautiful." Stanford grinned.

I sat to Stanford's right at the table, and he occupied the middle. With our limited knowledge of each other's languages, we engaged in a game of charades. First, I wrote the letter "S" on a piece of lined sand-colored paper, and then I had him trace it. In this manner, I showed him how to write each letter of his name.

When it was his turn, he heaved a sigh, picked up the pencil with his stiff seventy-nine-year-old fingers, and began to write the letter "S." If he hesitated with a letter, I took his hand with his index finger pointing down and helped him draw the letter. After he finished his name, I had him repeat the process a couple of times.

Following this, we worked on a Xhosa beginner book for adult non-readers, and then I read the first lesson of *Foundational Teachings of the Bible* by Isiseko Sezifundo Zebhayible in Xhosa. I hoped this would help him with his sermons, devotions, and messages. Whenever I struggled with a word, Stanford smiled and pronounced it properly. I knew I amused him with my mispronunciation of syllable accents on certain words, but he seemed grateful for my efforts.

As time passed, Stanford continued to inspire me. Sometimes when I drove on the gravel road that led to the church, I found him walking from the government health clinic. Each Wednesday morning, he delivered devotions there. Since the clinic was a great distance from his home, I offered him a ride. As we drove to his church, he told me in Xhosa what scripture he had read to the people that day.

This spry little man, who walked to other preaching stations in the Ciskei, reminded me of Caleb, an Old Testament spy and warrior. At age eighty-five, Caleb took possession of the hill country of Canaan.

In June of 1995, God used Stanford in a mighty way when he preached the sermon for the funeral of Colbin and Sylvia Ngonyama. At the time of his death, Colbin served at a church in Butterworth, Transkei. A dynamic Xhosa evangelist, Colbin was sixty-two-years-old and his wife Sylvia fifty-seven.

During our lesson that day, Stanford related the events of the Ngonyama's tragic deaths. While driving home on a mountain road, the couple's car was forced off a cliff with a 250-foot drop. Their deaths created shock waves throughout the Ciskei and the Transkei.

At their funeral, Stanford preached from John 5:24: "I tell you the truth, whoever hears my word and believes Him who sent me has eternal life and will not be condemned; he has crossed over from death to life." At the conclusion of the funeral, Stanford invited the people to respond to the message. Twenty-four individuals came forward and received Jesus as Lord and Savior.

After my class with Stanford, I helped Winfred, his wife, or Winnie as she was called. At our first encounter, she was wearing a long pink and black flowered dress with a white coat. A black doek, something similar to a beret, covered her head. At age fifty-three, she was short and sturdy. She blossomed as a pastor's wife and mother to her and Stanford's six children.

I discovered Winnie understood and read English, but needed help with listening and communication skills and with language structure. I asked her to listen to English radio programs for ten minutes a day to strengthen her listening skills. To assist with communication and language structure, I requested that she write how she became a Christian.

Later, on her own initiative, Winnie started a Xhosa literacy class with nine ladies at Ndevana, a neighboring village. Four of the ladies were over sixty and had never attended school.

Winnie continued teaching the ladies even though I left for a three-month trip to the United States. When I returned, Winnie asked me to visit the class. "Some of them can read in Xhosa now," she whispered with a proud expression.

"They can read in Xhosa?" I replied, raising my eyebrows suspiciously.

"Yes!"

"And before you started teaching them, they could not read at all?"

"No!"

"Have they been to school before?"

"They have *never* been to school," Winnie stated firmly. "Shumikazi can read this book!" She pointed to a book.

Shumikazi sat on one of the four benches at the communion table. Winnie asked her to read for me. Her seventy-year-old chocolate face sparkled, and her black eyes glowed as she opened the book and started to read. I later discovered the intelligence of this tall lady as I taught her English as a second language. She could have earned a doctorate at any university in the world if only she had been given the opportunity. Silently, I grieved for Shumikazi and the ladies who had been denied an education.

As our classes continued, I noticed the ladies were not making the progress I had expected. I soon realized some had trouble distinguishing the small print. One little lady over age sixty used the right side of a pair of glasses to read. Other ladies could not see the print because of poor vision.

To help solve this dilemma, I visited my optometrist to see what could be done for the ladies. I learned the government had a program to provide glasses. I made arrangements for each lady to see the optometrist for an eye exam. This endeavor took two separate days.

As I suspected, they all needed glasses. Notembile had a white substance in front of her pupil and iris that required further testing at the eye clinic at Frere Hospital. Winnie went with us to translate. The tests revealed Notembile needed eye surgery. The doctor admitted her to the hospital. The surgery was successful, and Notembile was elated to see out of both eyes.

I was thrilled to see the progress the ladies made after getting glasses. Winnie also continued to do well teaching English. However, sometimes I worried about the way the women treated their glasses. One day, Shumikazi forgot hers. I couldn't help but think she might have broken them. Violet also kept leaving hers on a pew without the case. Thankfully, Nowinile and Notembile wore their glasses throughout the class time.

Later, I learned that Shumikazi, delighted with her ability to read, had taught Vina, her neighbor, how to read. One day she brought Vina to our class. Concerned about giving each lady enough attention, I was not eager to accept any new students in the class. But when I tested Vina and saw her progress, I felt confident enough to add her to the class roll.

In order to further enhance the literacy ministry, I began bringing a mobile library with Bible storybooks, both in Xhosa and English that I had purchased from the Bible Society. Every week, each lady could check out two of the books. They would look at their books and decipher the words of the title. They were faithful to both check out and return the books.

Over time, Winnie and I shared many experiences and developed a strong bond. I thanked the Lord for allowing me to be a part of this ministry that transformed the lives of so many individuals. But my most rewarding moments occurred before each literacy class. Gathered around the communion table, Winnie would lead a Bible study while I witnessed the ladies reading and learning to use their Bibles. I enjoyed helping them find their way among the sixty-six books of the Old and New Testaments. They could find and read a verse anywhere in the Bible. Illumination had finally come to the people of Tshabo.

Chapter Twenty-One

THE YOUTH AT DONGWE

It is the Lord your God you must follow, and him you must revere. Keep his commands and obey him; serve him and hold fast to him.
Deuteronomy 13:4

At Dongwe, on a summer morning in 1996, we could see a little white church sitting atop a hill. The worship services were in Xhosa, and since neither Gene nor I was fluent, we had some trepidation about trying to help the congregation. It would require Gene to preach in English, and then a translator would translate what he said, making the service twice as long. Further, our company had assigned us to English-speaking ministries. This meant we had no dedicated time to learn the language, although we managed to complete one short Xhosa class at the local college.

However, after we visited the church that first Sunday, I noticed several young people and thought I could lead them in some type of study.

The next Sunday, as we drove up the hill, many people recognized us and waved. We arrived at 10:00 a.m. so I could lead the youth class. A few minutes after ten, we only had three youths. I had asked them to arrive by ten, but I practiced patience, remembering once again that the people were more event-oriented than time conscious. By 10:45 a.m., we had at least twelve in attendance.

One conscientious boy stood up and apologized for the teens arriving late. He said that my teaching would be a good experience for them, and that they would be on time the following week.

Because I wanted to know if each teenager was a Christian or would hopefully become one, I first went through an evangelistic tract entitled "Do You Know for Certain That You Are a Christian and That You Will Go to Heaven When You Die?" I was happy to learn later that eight had made a profession of faith and awaited baptism. I asked each student to take the tract home and share it with their family and friends.

Since the tin roof had no insulation, the church was very hot. But rather than focusing on my discomfort, I was glad I could stand and teach this wonderful group of young people. I counted it a blessing to lead them to a closer walk with the Lord. And despite the heat, we had a wonderful class.

During the worship service, the men sat on one side, and the women sat on the other side, which was typical of Black churches. Up front, to the left of the pulpit, the youth sat in an area something like where choir members would sit. Since the church was at capacity, small children filled the center aisle.

The children's Sunday school teacher, a young woman, had taught the children the song, "My Heavenly Father Watches Over Me." They sang it beautifully during the service. Umfundisi Wellington Tela, the pastor, announced how good the attendance was and that it was the best since he had become pastor.

The next Sunday when we reached Dongwe, we saw that the church windows and front door were open. Gene and I were delighted at the sight and were grateful to the four young men who had come early to open the church. Never before had we encountered such advance preparation. Usually the door was locked.

For each of our Sunday visits, I would normally go to the manse first with a bag of groceries that contained food items such as rice, bread, tea, sugar, coffee, and CoffeeMate. Each time we came, Nosithabo, the pastor's wife, served us something to drink and eat. On this day, I heard a radio and saw her down on her knees, waxing the kitchen floor.

After enjoying the refreshments, I went to the church and started the youth class with four young men present. Soon, two girls came in. By the end of the hour, I counted twelve. I checked their books to see if they had completed the work. Happily, they had. As a former schoolteacher, I believe in accountability.

Our Bible study focused on Galatians 5:22-23, the fruit of the Holy Spirit. And what a fruitful class we had along with a marvelous time in the presence of the Lord! It was by far one of the most enjoyable classes I had led in South Africa. That particular morning, I had come to Dongwe emotionally and spiritually depleted. I just wanted to get through the class and leave, but the Lord filled my heart, soul, and mind overflowing with His Holy Spirit. He had heard my prayers for serving Him joyfully in this church.

As the class ended, I had the youth sing from the Baptist Hymnal, "What a Friend We Have in Jesus" and "The Church's One Foundation," followed by my favorite hymn, "When We All Get to Heaven." I shared how I looked forward to heaven where we could all understand each other.

We continued to sing hymns for the next hour, and they seemed in no hurry to leave. A student named Lindile requested that we sing "When We All Get to Heaven" again to help him learn the verses. The youth had wonderful voices, and I loved the way they harmonized together. As we sang, many children came and sat quietly, listening. We kept singing since there was no worship service that day due to a funeral.

I had learned that Black pastors considered funerals the biggest barrier to their ministries. People would walk miles to attend funerals. Funerals also occurred on Sundays in many places. With people attending funerals instead of church, sometimes services were canceled. On occasion, when we traveled to other towns for church services, we witnessed funeral processions in progress.

The next time I met with the youth, there were only three in attendance for the entire class period. I was tempted to be discouraged until I recalled the circumstances of the two previous weekends—cancellation of services due to a funeral, and later, my own absence due to other ministry needs. I knew a lack of consistency hurt the church and its ministries.

Later, when the worship service started at 11:00 a.m., only a few people sat in the pews. But as time progressed, I looked out a window and noticed more people coming. Minutes later, a crowd filled the pews and chairs.

On this particular Sunday, we took a cake for the wedding anniversary celebration of Umfundisi Wellington and his wife Nositabo. A few minutes before the youth class ended, the couple arrived, nicely dressed. Gene and I felt they honored and brought glory to the Lord through their faithful work and church ministries. Truly, they were "following the Master" in reverence, obedience, and service.

CHAPTER TWENTY-TWO

MINISTRY AT BUBELE

*If anyone serves Me, let him follow Me: and where
I am, there My servant will be also. If anyone
serves Me, him My Father will honor.*
John 12:26

"Molo, Umfundisi!" Joel Cweba beamed. I could tell he had some good news for us. We'd been asked to help the Bubele Church in the Mulangisa township near Stutterheim, fifty miles north of East London. Joel was the pastor. Tall with short black hair and wearing a pink shirt and striped tie, he looked handsome in a light brown suit.

Just after Gene returned his greeting, Joel blurted out, "A piano has been donated to our church by a lady in Stutterheim."

When I heard this, I was determined not to let my face show what I was thinking. In the past, I had seen pianos donated to churches that were in miserable condition. From across the room, I could tell the piano had been denied a proper death. I walked up smiling anyway and sat down on the bench, but Joel announced, "It must be dusted first." An individual produced a cloth and dusted the poor thing as directed.

It looked like it had sat outside for years. The music holder was loose and protruded outwards. Most of the top white pieces of the keys were also missing, and the black ones were a dark-weathered gray. When I started to play, I heard a board, apparently attached to the face of the piano, fall across the hammers inside. Nevertheless, I played as though the piano was a baby grand, pounding the keys to make music.

During the service, the people seemed thrilled to have a piano in their midst. I looked out to see their smiles and enjoyed hearing their voices, raised in beautiful harmony. They sang from their hearts with reverence, revealing their love for God.

Later in October, however, a disturbing event occurred during a service. Gene had just shown the second part of the Jesus film and one person accepted Christ. Joel walked to the pulpit to lead in a closing prayer. As he finished, a man barged in and shouted, "Ndiza kubulala (*I'll shoot you!*)"

I sat next to Constance, Joel's wife, on the front pew. Constance turned to me and asked, "Did you hear the man say he would fight Joel?"

"No, I did not understand what he said."

"He said, 'I'll shoot you.'"

"You mean Joel!" I was flabbergasted and heard pandemonium break out.

"Yes!"

I turned to glance at Makabongwe, the pastor's son, sitting with his friends on our pew. He looked visibly shaken and hurried to leave.

As if in a trance, Joel stood behind the pulpit, not knowing what to do or to say. Thankfully, the man left. After the service, Gene and I walked with Joel and Constance to the manse next door for lunch.

I learned Makabongwe had gone to his bedroom and cried. His father went to comfort him. When Joel came to the living room, he told us what Makabongwe had said: "I don't like this thing."

With a weary sigh, Joel told us, "This man could hire someone to shoot me. He is a businessman in the community. Some people have stopped coming to the church because of him."

This news was discouraging. Almost every Sunday, the church saw someone profess Christ, but this businessman and former deacon complicated things with his hateful words. It seemed his action was precipitated by a report from the annual regional meeting in Queenstown the day before. The report dealt with the removal of members from the church roll.

We also learned that a mediator had helped every pastor at the Bubele Church deal with this man. At one point, he had been the church treasurer and would not give the pastor his salary, R500 or about $100. The man even resisted turning over the financial records to the church. Finally, when the church obtained the books from him, they discovered he had stolen church funds.

After we had counseled and prayed with this dedicated pastoral couple, we left for East London. When we arrived home, Gene called Umfundisi Michael Limba, a Black pastor, who was president of the Border United Baptist Association. He would help Joel decide how to handle the matter.

In addition to the problem with the former deacon, Joel's family did not live together. Joel and Makabongwe lived in the manse in Mulungisa, a four-year-old son lived two hours away with his grandmother, and during the week, Constance lived with their sixteen-year-old daughter in Mdantsane, not far from East London. While their daughter attended school in the township, Constance worked in East London. After Constance finished work on Saturday afternoon at 1:00 p.m., she traveled to Mulungisa to be with her husband and son. On Sunday afternoon, she returned to Mdantsane. Her efforts to find a job closer to Joel had failed. Regrettably, this statistic was the norm among the Xhosa people as they eked out a living under the most trying circumstances.

*

Rrrrrrrrrring! The alarm signaled that it was 4:00 a.m.—time to get up and prepare to go to Mulungisa. We left a few minutes after five o'clock on November 17, 1996, a spring day, and hoped to reach the church by six o'clock for a baptism. The people from Dakana would walk over four miles across the mountains to attend the baptism. The church members had also spent the night in the church building for an all-night prayer and praise meeting. No one slept.

Due to fog on the road, we drove slower and didn't arrive until 6:10 a.m. When we reached the church yard, some people had already started for the Kubusie River since they assumed we weren't coming.

On that cloudy day, a steady rain fell and continued the entire morning as we trudged down to the river. With the swift current and the temperature at 9 degrees Celsius (38 degrees Fahrenheit), I had concern for the people getting baptized, but fourteen of the twenty-two candidates decided to brave the elements anyway.

In my teal weather coat, boots, and plastic rain scarf, I carried a small umbrella while Gene and the pastor used our large umbrella. Since our entourage of fifty people, including women, men, and children, only had eight umbrellas, we huddled together as we walked and sang praise songs. Villagers stood in their doorways, watching us pass and listening.

The pastor sent runners ahead to find the best place for the baptisms since the waters were too swift at the regular location. I wondered why they didn't postpone baptisms when the weather was cold and rainy, but I again reminded myself that Africans were more event-oriented.

The water was so cold that the candidates appeared to be in shock. After a couple of people had been immersed, I handed my purse to Constance and slipped down the side of the bank to help the candidates out. The pastor would baptize one and then turn to the next candidate. One older lady flailed about. I got as near to her as I dared and reached out my right arm to help her. She pulled so hard, I feared she would pull me in. During the struggle, I felt something give in my shoulder muscle. Several months later, after surgery and physical therapy, my shoulder healed. Looking back, I probably should have let her pull me into the water.

On the way back, we once again sang praise songs and soon enjoyed refreshments at the church. By 8:00 a.m., Gene and I were at the manse. It felt great to feel the heat and smell the odor of the kerosene heater while drying off. As we warmed ourselves, Constance said, "The church has prepared the letter."

Earlier Lionel Grunewald, the coordinator of the border area, encouraged the church to write and send a letter to the man who had threatened Joel. It would be hand-delivered that day.

We visited with the Cweba couple a while longer and then left for the Stutterheim church. Gene was to preach since the church had no pastor. Concerned about the impact of the letter, Joel and Constance asked Gene to come back after the Stutterheim service.

Later when we arrived back at Bubele Church around 11:45 a.m., the church was observing the Lord's Supper. We entered quietly and sat near the back of the church. It would be 1:00 p.m. before the service ended. But the ex-deacon had brought four men with him and came inside the building.

People began leaving. Gene accompanied Joel outside to check the church grounds. Gene then asked, "Is it all right for me to leave now?" Apprehensive, Joel asked him to stay longer. After a short while, they went back into the church. Thankfully, nothing happened with the ex-deacon and his men. They soon stood up and left. Gene's presence seemed to have bought Joel extra time to handle the matter. The man kept causing trouble, but thankfully, left the church soon afterwards.

In the following months, Joel continued to shepherd the church as a faithful servant of Jesus. Gene and I admired him immensely. Not only did he remain steadfast as a pastor, but he continued to minister while undergoing great trials.

Chapter Twenty-Three

AN UNINVITED VISITOR

*The angel of the Lord encamps around those
who fear him, and he delivers them.*
Psalm 34:7

"Gene! Come quick," I called from the hallway. "I think *that thing* is in our guest room." I had walked by the door en route to our bedroom when I heard a rustling behind some boxes. Returning, I noticed the skirt ruffle of the small bedside table moving. I then saw a shiny black creature that looked like a huge snake. I watched for a second and quickly shut the door. Gene opened the door to see for himself.

"Don't open the door too wide. I don't want that thing getting lost in the house!"

The day before, Heidi, our German shepherd, had treed *that thing* in the backyard. *That thing* was a leguaan, a large lizard species from the reptile class, that measured about three feet in length and six inches in diameter. When we first came to South Africa, we had been warned about this huge lizard.

I then saw the leguaan on our lush green grass and watched Gene chase it with a stick to our back fence. It crawled onto some small tree branches that hung over into the neighbor's backyard and disappeared. I felt relieved that Gene had been able to chase it away.

David, the neighbor across the street, had followed the lizard to our yard to warn us about it. "You'll find that in the morning it'll be gone," he said. Before he left, he added, "You don't have to worry. They never come in your house."

Somebody forgot to tell the leguaan that.

When I had called Gene after spotting the leguaan in our guest room, he was getting ready to attend a Home Mission Committee meeting at 2:30 p.m. It was a few minutes after two o'clock and his ride would be coming for him soon.

Nevertheless, he called several people to see what we should do. Finally, he called the zoo, and they gave him the number of Mr. Schultz, who caught animals for a living. Mr. Schultz would come if we paid him.

Anticipating the need for backup, I called our neighbor David and his mother Jill. Fifteen minutes later, Mr. Schultz arrived. He wore an animal society uniform, a long leather glove on his left hand, and black boots.

He entered the guest room with cloth bags while David, Jill, and I stood outside the door and waited. When we heard scuffling on the carpet, I called out, "Are you all right?"

"It bit me," Mr. Schulz answered.

There was more scuffling. "Do you need help?"

"I can't get him in the sack. Could two of you open the bag and hold it for me so I can put it in?"

With my heart pounding, I opened the door. David reached for the bag. Mr. Schultz held the leguaan's head with his left hand and both a front and back leg with his right hand. Its other front and back leg thumped the floor. Thankfully, David and I held the bag open wide enough for Mr. Schultz to put the monster in. He then laid the bag on the floor with the top twisted several times and said, "She'll settle down in the sack."

She?

For a moment, he was quiet, but then added, "I hesitate to tell you what else I caught in your bedroom—a rinkhals, which is a type of spitting cobra. It's lying in that sack on the bed and is about eighteen inches long. I caught it beside the drapes by the window."

During the interim, the leguaan had laid eggs and deposited feces. There was also a strong acid smell. Mr. Schultz further cautioned me, "You must get this cleaned up immediately because the acid will destroy the carpet, and the odor will attract the male.

He went on to add that this leguaan was the largest he had ever caught, and that he would need to seek medical treatment for his wound. He also informed us that he had been collecting reptiles and animals for twenty plus years and sent them to other countries. Thankfully, leguaans were not poisonous, even though they could bite and inflict damage with heavy blows of their tails.

I couldn't help but remember how earlier that morning I had stayed in the guest room from 6:00-7:00 a.m. for my quiet time. Neither the lizard nor the snake had been in the room during that time. They must have entered through the screenless window sometime between 7:00 a.m. and 2:00 p.m. The Lord was watching over me.

Throughout our years in South Africa, we continued to experience His protection and presence. Whether it was from dangerous animals or dangerous circumstances, God was faithful to deliver us.

CHAPTER TWENTY-FOUR

A TREASURED FRIENDSHIP IN CAPE TOWN

Be devoted to one another in love.
Honor one another above yourselves.
Romans 12:10

After we had served in East London for nine years, Gene became the director of Theological Education by extension for Cape Town Baptist College (now Cape Town Baptist Seminary). I served as his secretary.

On January 27, 1997, we left our beloved East London home and ministry for this new assignment. During the first few months, we organized and operated the program out of our home before we could move to the college. At this point, we were three years away from our final stateside assignment and retirement.

We didn't have much time to get to know our new neighbors. In order to meet them, we would take an early walk each morning with our dog Heidi. Some months after we'd started this routine, a ten-year-old girl, Miriam,[13] began to walk with me. A talkative girl, I enjoyed having her along because Gene and Heidi walked faster and stayed out in front.

Miriam would meet us by our gate on her way to school. One morning, I inquired about her religious persuasion and her church. She said that she was partly Christian, but also associated with another world religion. Since she didn't want to talk about spiritual things, I let the matter rest and focused on developing a good relationship with her.

One particular morning, she arrived at our gate clearly upset and could not wait to talk to me. A schoolmate had witnessed to her about spiritual things and told her she was going to burn in hell. The girl also demanded that Miriam "look it up since it was in the Bible." Miriam refused to do so.

I knew this was a critical moment. I prayed for wisdom and replied gently, "As a child of the Lord, He is responsible for my care. The Bible tells me each day of my life is scheduled by Him."

Miriam opened up about her late maternal grandmother who had been a Christian. She had witnessed to Miriam and taught her how to pray. The woman had also been a diabetic and had one of her legs amputated. Still, she was an optimist.

---

[13] Name has been changed.

She called her stump "Sunny." When Miriam's grandmother was in the hospital dying, she told Miriam that she was going to a beautiful place and would not need legs since she would have wings. The woman further told Miriam not to cry.

"But it's all right to cry when we lose a loved one," I said in a gentle voice.

"It's hard to cry now," Miriam said. "I guess it's because I'm bitter."

"If you're bitter, you must be angry at something or someone."

"Yes, I am."

"Do you know who you're angry with?" I expected to hear Miriam say she was angry with God since that was a typical answer.

"I'm angry with my father. He's mean to my mother." She went on to tell me her parents divorced when she was in sub-B (second grade). Afterwards, she and her mother lived with her father's parents who were members of a world religion. She said it was hard to be a Christian and live with them. I heard despair in her voice.

A few months later, Miriam moved five blocks away to a residence that was closer to her school. I was sad when she moved.

God brings precious souls in and out of our lives. How I treasured the times Gene and I walked each morning with Miriam, and I hoped my friendship helped her. But later I realized something else: the Lord had given me a special gift in this little girl, for she was like a granddaughter to me, the exact age as my own granddaughter, Laura Beth.

CHAPTER TWENTY-FIVE

LADIES SEMINAR

*Let us then approach the throne of grace with
confidence, so that we may receive mercy and
find grace to help us in our time of need.*
Hebrews 4:16

From my earliest days in South Africa, I enjoyed attending the ladies seminar each year. Promoted by the South Africa Baptist Women's Department (SABWD), it normally met at different venues across the country. In 1999, we assembled at Aventura Hotel near the Gariep Dam, a beautiful lake surrounded by mountains. Euphoria reigned among our ladies because Jill Briscoe from the United States was coming to speak. The attendance had grown each year, and now three hundred women had registered for 1999. They came from all over the country, and a large group had come from Walvis Bay, Namibia, a two days' drive.

As president of the SABWD for the current year, I was responsible for giving the devotions each morning and evening. Jill, the plenary speaker, spoke on "Prayer That Works" and led us to the throne of grace in a magnificent way. Her messages reached the hearts of the ladies, helping them experience God more fully.

One of the most significant illustrations Jill gave centered on Prime Minister Winston Churchill and Dunkirk during World War II. The Allies, representing British, French, and Belgium governments, had retreated to the beach of Dunkirk. Hundreds of thousands of Allied troops were caught and cornered on this beach in France because they had underestimated the strength of the German army. Further, the harbor was partially blocked by sunken ships. Facing a horrific catastrophe, the prime minister and the people of Britain prayed. For some mysterious reason, instead of attacking the Allies by land, Adolf Hitler ordered his generals to stop for three days. The "halt order" gave the Allies time to attempt an evacuation of the troops at Dunkirk. Despite constant bombardment by German fighter and bomber planes, the Allies rescued over 330,000 Allied troops with an amateur armada of ships, civilian boats, and paddle steamers. If this rescue had not happened, the British army would have been destroyed, and Nazi Germany might have won the war. This event became known as The Miracle of Dunkirk.[14]

---

[14] Britannica, The Editors of Encyclopaedia. "Dunkirk evacuation". Encyclopedia Britannica, 16 Sep. 2024, https://www.britannica.com/event/Dunkirk-evacuation. Accessed 26 September 2024.

One of the devotions I gave centered on forgiveness. I shared how Gene and I had lost a church many years ago and how I had struggled to forgive those responsible. I focused on the prayer Jesus prayed for those who nailed Him to the cross as the greatest depiction of forgiveness the world would ever see. "Father, forgive them, for they do not know what they are doing" (Luke 23:24).

I furthered shared steps to forgiveness through writings by Alexander C. DeJong, a minister and former president of Trinity Christian College, and Lewis B. Smedes, author, theologian, and professor at Fuller Theological Seminary.

DeJong wrote that forgiveness involved three things: foregoing the right to strike back, replacing the feeling of resentment and anger with good will, and taking concrete steps to restore good relations. (Alexander C. DeJong, "Leadership," Vol. 4, no 1.)

From the Lewis B. Smedes book, *Forgive & Forget*, I explained the four necessary stages of the forgiving process: The first stage was "the hurt" which created a crisis that felt "personal, unfair, and deep." An individual would keep replaying the hurt. In my case with our lost church, I kept hearing words that had been said.

Hate was the natural response to "any deep and unfair pain." An individual might want the offender to suffer. The hurt might also create bitterness, a callused heart, and an inability to love and sympathize with others. But the Christian had the ultimate resource to handle hate: God's help and prayer. Hate led to the third stage: healing.

Healing involved a shifting of focus from the offender to the wounded forgiver, and would require "spiritual surgery" that cut away the offense. An individual must then let the offense go like a child who opens his hand and sets a trapped butterfly free. Then it became time to invite the offender back into a relationship.

The fourth stage was the reunion, "the flight to freedom," when the individuals came together, but it required honesty and truthfulness. And sometimes, forgiveness was a "solo flight."

I ended my devotion by sharing that unforgiveness is a luxury we cannot afford as Christians. When we refuse to forgive, we sabotage our own life and ministry. Whatever comes into our lives, God trusts us to handle it appropriately.

During the seminar, one memorable event that took place was a power outage during an afternoon session. We learned the problem was not in the building, but at the municipality. With no sound system, Carol Crutchley, our musician for the week, led the group a cappella. When the time came for Jill to speak, she said, "Carry on singing. I can't speak without a sound system." As the women sang, Margie Martin and I prayed for God to show *His* power and to show us what to do. Lesley Brandt, the South Africa Baptist Women's Director, soon told me about a new plan: Jill would lead groups of ladies in prayer.

After our prayer time, we were dismissed until 5:30 p.m. Jill and I returned to our rooms. Immediately, she sat down at her desk and began writing. I thought, *I'll turn the light on for her*, forgetting momentarily that it wouldn't do any good.

I returned to my room, troubled by the power outage. It had derailed our plans. With few options, I opened the sliding door of the patio and went outside. Standing in the cool autumn breeze, I saw dark clouds hanging over the lake. I sat down and glanced at the hills and sky. Soon, rays of light shone through the clouds. I sensed the Lord speaking to my troubled heart. "Be still and know that I am God."

Time came to return to the hall. After I went in, I discovered that Eric Robbins, the mission leader for South Africa, had presented Bible Way, a Bible Study program. I also heard the ladies asking him questions. Then it dawned on me what God had wanted to show us while we were "in the dark"—the Bible Way program. With nothing to do or places to go, the ladies heard this in-depth Bible study. Thankfully, the electricity came back on at twilight.

Following the evening meal, we continued an earlier board meeting. A while later, Pat Ilenfeld, the current director of SABWD, came into the room and said they were ready for Ellamae. I left to go and speak to the ladies in the general assembly as Irene Rutter, our new president-elect, took over the board meeting. Before I spoke, an energetic and joyful group of Xhosa women came up to the platform and sang "Soon and Very Soon We Are Going to Meet the King".

God will not be stopped by a mere power outage. Throughout the week, He was glorified as we met together for prayer, messages, devotions, and fellowship. Further, standing in queues during mealtimes, ladies shared stories of how God had worked in their lives. They shared stories of answered prayers. Truly, God had met us in our time of need with His mercy and grace.

Chapter Twenty-Six

TWO WEEKS OF WONDER

I will sing of the Lord's great love for ever;
with my mouth I will make Your faithfulness
known through all generations.
Psalm 89:1

Little did I know when I returned to East London how magnificent the next two weeks would be. Previously, on June 4, the country had held the second free election. I was concerned about traveling during this time. News sources had predicted more chaotic days. Thankfully, the election proceeded without much trouble and certainly not with the deaths that led up to the first democratic election of 1994. Mtabo Mbeki was elected president to succeed President Nelson Mandela.

The day following my arrival, Oscarina met me at the Duplessis's residence, and we traveled by car to Idutywa, formerly the Transkei, for the Eastern Baptist Women's Department Rally (BWD).

We had a safe trip and saw only a few wild drivers. In the Kei cuttings, a curvy area of the road, there was no traffic. At the last Kei cutting toward Butterworth, I learned how and where Colben and Sylvia Nganyomas had died. When another car entered their lane head-on, they were forced off the road as they traveled home.

At Idutywa, two hundred ladies from the former Ciskei and Transkei gathered in the downtown municipal hall. They sat on benches with no backs and spent the night there. They were afraid to leave the building to go to the homes of the local ladies of the Baptist Women's Department. There would not have been sufficient hotel accommodations for these ladies even if they could have afforded the prices.

As a nurse talked during the Saturday night session, around 6 p.m. a storm caused the lights to flicker. It was wintertime and cold in the building. Within a few minutes, the lights went out, and in the darkness, the ladies stood and sang. When a time of prayer followed, the ladies prayed audibly.

During the testimony time, one lady shared how she was saved at her sister-in-law's funeral. Her parents and friends were angry that she had become a Christian because they had lost a drinking buddy. She always carried a Bible even though her friends knew she'd never attended school and couldn't read. Now she was learning how to read.

Around 6:20 p.m., a lady passed out candles. I was constantly amazed how Black services continued, regardless of circumstances and in this case, with no electricity. Throughout the rally, I heard many inspirational messages as Oscarina translated for me. Eventually, the electricity came back on.

Two days later, I left East London at 11:00 a.m. on a double-decker bus. My seat was on the second level, for which I was delighted. I could see the countryside as we traveled. We pulled into an ultra-Shell station on the outskirts of Umtata at 2:50 p.m. I couldn't believe how fast and quickly we had made this trip. The roads were narrow and curvy with lots of potholes, animals, and people.

Johannie Goss, the pastor of Maclear Church, and his wife Margaret met me at the station. As we drove off, I experienced the fastest car ride of my life. I sat in the back seat and avoided looking at the speedometer because I didn't need to know how fast we were flying. Instead, I remembered how the Lord had assured me He would keep me safe as I traveled.

Over dinner that night, Margaret related how their family came to faith in Christ. Johannie was an athlete. Out running one day, he fell and blacked out while hearing the words, "Where would you go if you had to die now?" (A Damascus Road experience!) For two days, he walked around in a stupor since he could not visit with a pastor. Afterwards, the pastor of the Methodist Church told him how to be become a Christian. When Johannie returned home, Margaret could tell he was different, but his salvation experience caused tension between them.

But on Easter Sunday of that same year, Margaret accepted Christ. A month later, their eight-year-old daughter Debbie made the same decision, and a month after that, their five-year-old son Johnny also accepted Christ. The Lord then called Johannie into the ministry, and the family relocated so he could attend Cape Town Baptist Seminary.

When I met the Gosses, Johannie had been a pastor for over nine years. A month before, he had been diagnosed with Parkinson's disease. Shortly afterwards, their daughter and son who lived in Durban had an accident on their return trip from visiting their parents. They sensed the Lord holding their car upright to prevent a rollover, thus sparing their lives.

One morning, Margaret and I had tea with Joy, a lady who had myeloma. A year earlier, she had lost her eldest son Elwin in an accident, and three years before that she had lost her youngest son Glenn. Consumed with grief, Elwin's wife Lynn would not visit her mother-in-law. Her right arm had also been mangled in the accident, and she had only regained thirty percent of its use. In addition to her physical disability, she had the pressure of running the family business. And to make matters worse, Joy had been bedridden from May to November of the previous year with what the doctors thought was osteoporosis. How this family needed hope and healing. Happily, during our visit, Lynn arrived, and Joy and Lynn reconciled right before our eyes as we drank tea from Royal Doulton china.

Back at Margaret's home, she told me about an eighteen-year-old boy who was on track to complete two final exams to finish high school. Sadly, he was tragically killed in a truck accident. His friend, who had been drinking and driving, was not injured. One Sunday morning soon afterwards, the family of the deceased boy came to the Maclear church service and sat in the front. The young man who had been driving the truck also came in and sat with them. He began to weep. The pastor went to help him, and the Holy Spirit took over. The deceased boy's family hugged the distraught young man, and they forgave him for his part in the accident. Margaret said with eloquence, "The Lord did open-heart surgery on the family." At the time, the mother knew Christ, but the father didn't.

However, two weeks later, the boy's father had a dream in which the Lord showed him two coffins. One was his wife who was ready to meet the Lord and the other, his own coffin. The Lord told the father that He didn't know him. The man awoke at 3:00 a.m. and waited for daylight. He then appeared at the pastor's home trembling and told him that he needed to get his life in order. The pastor explained the plan of salvation, and the father came to Christ.

All too soon, my visits with Margaret and the ladies at Maclear ended. I had been inspired and encouraged to hear about and see God's miraculous presence and work. It was time for me to return to the Shell station in Umtata to catch the bus. Since we had waited rather late to begin the return trip, I knew I would have another wild ride.

Back in East London, I left for speaking engagements in Gompo township on Saturday and Sunday, where I used a translator. How I loved visiting the Mashologu Church again, which held many memories.

I also attended the District BWD meeting and visited with many friends. What a blessing to see how the BWDs had grown through ongoing ministries that helped others and shared the gospel. Being in East London again put "the icing on the cake."

On another day, Oscarina took me to the new senior citizens' building in Gompo. The group of ladies whom I had led in Bible and sewing classes years ago at Mashologu Church now met in this new building. I was thrilled to see them and hear about the many sewing classes that had sprung up. All over this big township, women heard the good news of Christ.

After I gave a devotion and we ate, Oscarina and I hurried to Tshabo church where I had held literacy classes. As we traveled on this late fall day, we smelled smoke from the burning of fields and pastures. Upon arriving, we welcomed ladies who had come from a nearby village where we had conducted other classes. What a grand reunion! It was wonderful to see their smiles and hear their laughter and once again challenge them to share the gospel.

For those two weeks in 1999, I was filled with a sense of wonder as I witnessed what the Lord had done. From the time we arrived in South Africa to our final days, He had multiplied our efforts and those of His devoted servants one hundredfold. I couldn't keep quiet. My heart sang of His great love and faithfulness.

Chapter Twenty-Seven

GOING HOME

Jesus…said, "Go home to your own people and tell them how much the Lord has done for you, and how He has had mercy on you."
Mark 5:19

On Friday, November 26, 1999, I wrote the following Scripture during my quiet time. "Putting to sea from there… We sailed slowly for a number of days, and arrived with difficulty…" (Acts 27:4, 7). We were leaving for the United States on November 28. I thought to myself, *Is this ominous statement meant for us?*

During our final days in South Africa, I felt guilty for not reaching out more to our neighbors. Homeless people lived under a bridge a short distance from our house. I asked Gene to go with me to visit these people. I packed two afghans I had crocheted, one green and blue, the other a multicolored one for an infant. In another bag, I placed religious tracts, Xhosa Bibles, and English New Testaments.

As we walked, I placed a tract in each mailbox along one side of our street. When we reached the trail to the bridge, we proceeded with caution. Soon we discovered four tattered mattresses and four makeshift shelters under the bridge. Flies covered the blankets that canopied the foul-smelling shelters. I placed the afghans on one mattress and the Bibles and Xhosa tracts on another.

As we walked back, Gene and I placed tracts in mailboxes on the opposite side of the street. But before going home, we stopped at a neighbor's house, two doors down from our house. Gee invited us in. A mother of four, Gee had lost her son two years earlier in a holdup. The thieves took R50,000 ($10,000) which was considered to be "the pickings of the day." The son left behind a wife and two children.

Gee's thirty-two-year-old daughter had also been diagnosed with cancer two years before this tragic event. Sadly, she died the same year as her brother. Gee had lost two children within a five-week period.

I asked Gee if she would like to have a religious tract. I followed up with the question,

"Do you know for certain that you have eternal life and that you will go to heaven when you die?" She was most appreciative of the tract. I prayed it would bring her into a personal relationship with Christ.

Guilt continued to plague me as we left Gee's house. I had lived in the community for three years, yet I had never visited her or others who lived nearby.

Back home, we packed our suitcases for the flight to the United States. All our things fit into four suitcases. When we finished, I had one last visit in mind. We took two upholstered throw pillows, a Bible, and a religious tract to our neighbors across the street. They belonged to another world religion and had always been friendly to us. I hope our actions made a difference.

On Sunday, we left for the Cape Town Airport to board a flight to Johannesburg. We greeted the families who came to wish us a bon voyage. Among the group were missionaries, people from our church, and students and professors from the seminary. There must have been over forty friends. It was also time to give our mission car keys to a colleague. The week before, we had sold our personal car. My key chain had become quite small—no house keys, no car keys, no burglar alarm keys. In fact, now I had no house or car.

After saying our goodbyes, we headed for the corridor that would take us to our gate. I still remember how energetically we walked, Gene carrying a heavy computer case while I held my carryon. We were in good health and our regular regimen of walking several miles per day had paid off. I was thankful as we left for the first leg of our long journey.

On that Sunday night, people swarmed the massive international waiting area of the Johannesburg airport—men wearing turbans and ankle-length tunics, mothers wearing head scarves, dresses and pants, clutching their little children's hands. Long lines stretched in front of the cafes and restaurants.

After Gene left to find food and drinks, a Black man came by to pick up pop cans at our table. He had a lovely smile. I felt led to give him a *Thank You* tract with the gospel message. He recognized the message, and his face lit up. I said, "You must be a Christian."

"Yes! A Methodist."

"We have been missionaries here and we're going back to the USA," I said.

"Why are you going?"

"The Lord has told us to go spend time with our children and grandchildren and to tell what He has done here."

"The Lord bless you as you go."

I appreciated his kindness. As he moved away, I saw Gene coming with two cans of pop. "This airport is out of food," he said. "I couldn't find any water. Only pop."

An hour later at midnight, the Alitalia plane, bound for Milan, groaned as we ascended into the dark night. Since our Johannesburg flight had been delayed, we didn't have time to enter the Milan airport. Instead, we dashed across the tarmac for our Continental flight to Newark, New Jersey.

On the eight-hour flight, Gene slept most of the way and never stood up. He seemed hot. Later when he asked for water,

I found the water fountain empty. I requested extra water from the flight attendant. She only gave me three small paper cups. Then she asked if we had a connecting flight and advised me to buy extra water for it. She also suggested Gene see the paramedic on board.

Looking back, I wish he had seen the paramedic at that time, but he refused. As we descended into Newark and taxied along the runway, I could hardly understand the soft-spoken pilot's update over the speakers, and I was growing anxious for Gene.

When we landed, we had to locate our luggage and proceed through customs. I couldn't find my large suitcase at baggage claim. The man at the information desk instructed me to make a claim upstairs.

Later, as we went through security for our next flight, Gene became disoriented. He didn't have his passport ready or his tickets out, and his money bag was unzipped. At one point during this ordeal, my nerves were so raw, I stood by a wall, crying. From the beginning, nothing seemed to work for our trip home. It had started off-kilter with our plane tickets, no food in the Johannesburg Airport, the delayed flight, exhaustion, and now Gene's illness. After flying on many pleasant international flights over the years, I found this one almost unbearable.

But in that hopeless place, God, in His mercy, sent angels to me in the form of a man and woman who were returning from a mission trip to South America. I told them Gene was sick, and we were retiring as South African missionaries and going home, but we still had two more flights.

The woman immediately answered, "Oh, you're suffering from culture shock."

The couple then took me by the hand, made a circle, and prayed for me.

On the flight to Denver, I noticed that Gene was worse. I talked to the flight attendant about his condition, and she arranged for a paramedic to meet our plane. We arrived at 7:20 p.m. The paramedics came on board with a wheelchair and took Gene to a large hallway to check him over.

I asked the paramedic, "What should he do?"

Turning to Gene, the man said, "I think we should ask the gentleman. What do you want to do?"

"Go to the motel," Gene replied.

Since our flight from Denver to Durango had been canceled due to fog, we received coupons for motel accommodations and new tickets for the flight to Durango the next day.

Quickly, I asked the paramedic, "What would you do if you were in his place?"

"I would check in with a physician."

"Then let's go!"

The paramedics placed Gene in a white ambulance with flashing lights that looked like the one on the television program *911*. I climbed in on the passenger side. I thought, *This can't be happening to us. It only happens on TV.* I also felt strange sitting on the passenger side. That was where we sat to drive a South African vehicle.

After a thirty-mile trip, we arrived at the downtown Denver Health Medical Center. The paramedics wheeled Gene into a small room in the huge emergency room department. I followed, tugging my carryon, the rest of my journals, and our computer.

A few minutes later, the doctor briefed us. "Due to an abnormal electrocardiogram, Gene should be admitted to the hospital," he said. "We need to find out what's causing this abnormality. His fever is 39.5 Celsius (103 Fahrenheit). Since you have traveled so far, we'll also check for blood clots."

Because Gene didn't get up to walk during the flights, he had also developed phlebitis in the calf of his right leg. I could hardly believe we were facing all these problems now, but the Lord brought these words to mind: "Endure hardship with us as a good soldier of Jesus Christ" (2 Timothy 2:3).

Around 10:30 p.m., I called our son David in New Mexico, and asked him to notify his siblings that Gene had been admitted to the hospital. At the time, Joy lived in Iowa and

Tim in Virginia. David knew we were grounded in Denver since the flight to Durango had been canceled.

Meanwhile, one test revealed a pulmonary embolism (blood clot) in Gene's right lung. On the plane, I had noticed his labored breathing like he was gasping for breath, but thought it was due to his fever. At 2:00 a.m., Gene was transported to a ward on the seventh floor. He shared a curtain space with one other patient.

Sitting by Gene that night, I wrote in my journal: *Lord, where are You? I can't pray, and I've been so afraid.*

The kind nurse wanted to put Gene in a private room, but explained that the hospital was full of flu patients. She did allow me to stay beside Gene and even brought me a pillow and blanket. I slept two hours in a straight-back chair since all the recliners were in use.

Later, I added the following prayer to my journal:

At this time, Lord, draw deep into my heart, mind, and soul and give me a greater, thankful heart in these trials. Help me to persevere with a thankful and joyous heart, and may it be evident to all people that I come in contact with today. Shower Your wisdom upon me.

I couldn't help but think back to the previous Friday, just a mere three days earlier, when I had pondered Acts 27. Like Paul in the New Testament, the winds had blown against us since before we had started our trip. And we had arrived "with difficulty" while time marched on. But five days later, by the grace of God, Gene walked out of the hospital.

After two more days of waiting, Gene and I sat in the Denver airport, bound for Durango. I grew anxious each time they announced a delay. Eventually however, we boarded, and the small plane ascended into the gray snow clouds. They grew darker and darker until we reached that glorious place where the sun was shining. We were going home to our family. We would tell them of the Lord's great mercy and how much He had done for us.

EPILOGUE

His master replied, 'Well done, good and faithful servant!
You have been faithful with a few things;
I will put you in charge of many things.
Come and share your master's happiness!'
Matthew 25:21

During our time in South Africa, we learned to trust the Lord for His direction, wisdom and provision to meet every need. As we reentered American life, that ongoing trust would sustain us through the coming year.

In January, during our final stateside assignment, we flew from Richmond, Virginia, to Chicago, Illinois. During the flight, Gene experienced numbness on his left side and was admitted to the hospital. A test revealed that a blood clot had caused a stroke. Thankfully, a few days later, he was discharged, and Joy drove us to her Iowa home. There, Gene completed physical therapy and successfully recovered, although he was left with residual deficiencies.

In February, we retired from the International Mission Board and relocated to my hometown of Greenville, Alabama.

At first, we lived in my parents' old farmhouse while our new house was constructed on land we had inherited. Our new house was nestled beside the woods with a pond close by. This acreage was like a retreat center. We enjoyed the quiet and hearing birds sing as well as watching the hummingbirds at our feeder. The front porch became a place to swing and observe nature. We felt most blessed by the Lord to live in this sanctuary.

Our children drove and flew long distances to visit us. When they came, laughter and joy rocked our house, and we made special memories.

One summer, Tim and his family traveled from their Richmond home. Seven-year-old Grace, her brother Luke, and Grandpa Gene went fishing in our pond. Soon, Grace felt a tug on her fishing pole. Gene told her to reel it in. Since she wasn't having much success, she turned with her back to the pond and marched up the bank until she had her fish out of the water. Over the years, untold family and friends spent hours enjoying good fishing in our pond.

With a desire to continue serving the Lord, we joined Southside Baptist Church and taught Sunday school. Gene taught the senior class, and I taught the tenth graders. I enjoyed singing in the choir, making friends, and joining other ministries. Gene also became a supply preacher for area churches.

One of our most fulfilling ministries was volunteering at the International Learning Center (ILC) in Rockville,

Virginia, where new missionary candidates prepared for assignments overseas. We supported these candidates and offered compassion and understanding as we ourselves had once needed before we went to South Africa. For several years, we traveled to ILC for three months. Volunteering at ILC was the cherry on top of a career in missions.

After we had been at Southside Church for several years, a new ministry opened. Sardis Baptist Church, a small fellowship near Greenville, asked Gene to serve as pastor.

A few years later, Gene had another health scare. One Sunday, he got up to preach. He had trouble reading the Bible. A church member asked him if he was all right. Gene responded, "No, I'm not all right." The service ended, and Gene and I left for the hospital.

The doctor examined Gene and warned, "This is the small stroke before the big one."

The doctor's warning came true in March of 2016, a time I will never forget. We attended the Alabama State Evangelism Conference in Montgomery. My March 7 birthday fell during the conference, yet we took time to celebrate it and returned home the next day.

Once home, my schedule returned to normal. However, one day later, just after lunch, I remember looking out the kitchen window to see Gene standing and viewing our property. Fatigued, I decided to rest. When I saw Gene again, he was lying on the sofa. He told me he had crawled home from getting the mail, a distance greater than five hundred feet.

Sadly, this was the big stroke. With this stroke, he lost his robust preaching voice and his vibrant personality. That day at the kitchen window was the last time I saw Gene strong and full of energy and ambition.

However, still somewhat driven, Gene rushed his recovery time and even returned to serving the Sardis Church. One lady had difficulty hearing him preach since the volume of his voice had decreased. After Gene's stroke, she sat on the front pew.

We served the Sardis Church for three more years, but trying to keep up our property was beginning to take its toll. Gene was now in his early eighties. In the spring and summer, he still mowed three acres every week. And while our wooded acreage was beautiful, we had tired of the huge job of raking and picking up leaves each fall. But we never thought of leaving our home. Gene even called our place the Done Roaming Ranch, declaring that he was done roaming. However, after seventeen years in Alabama, we sensed the Lord leading us to return to Aztec, where David and his family still lived.

We put our house on the market in 2018. After eleven months, it sold, and in the fall of 2019, once again, movers carted our things away.

Back in Aztec, we rejoined First Baptist Church. It was a wonderful homecoming. Many friends were still there from those years when Gene had pastored the church.

Our homecoming also meant enjoying nine of our great-grandchildren who lived nearby. We even moved in next door to our granddaughter, Jeannie, and her family. In 1987, when we left family, church, and country, Jeannie was two and a half years old. And now, here we were living next door to her. God had sheltered us, not only in South Africa, but also in Alabama, and now He had brought us full circle, back to Aztec. Only the Lord could arrange such an outcome.

On November 4, 2021, after suffering a long illness and living in an imprisoned body for many years, my beloved Gene left this world to go home to His Lord and Savior, Jesus Christ. He proved faithful and now shares in the joys of heaven. The Master says of these, "Well done, good and faithful servant." Oh, how I miss my husband, but I rejoice that he is experiencing eternal life.

My story isn't quite over yet. My heart still stirs with a call to share the gospel. Months after Gene passed away, I ordered a double headstone for our combined cemetery plot. On the headstone, I chose the scripture, "And you shall know the truth, and the truth shall set you free" (John 8:32). When the headstone was ready, I arranged to meet the two men who would install it. On that bright sunny day in August, 2022, I had the privilege, once again, of sharing the truth that would set these men free.

How about you, dear reader? Do you know the truth—that Christ died to set you free from sin? "If you declare with your mouth, 'Jesus is Lord,' and believe in your heart that God raised him from the dead, you will be saved" (Romans 10:9-10).

And if you already know this truth, are you sharing it with others? I can promise you that no matter what God calls you to do, even if it's to leave your family, your friends, and your country, you will dwell in the shelter of the Most High and will rest in the shadow of the Almighty.

To God be all glory

www.ingramcontent.com/pod-product-compliance
Lightning Source LLC
Chambersburg PA
CBHW060521100426
42743CB00009B/1395

Ellamae Elder's book, *In His Shelter,* is full of adventure and "God Stories." After twenty-six years of ministry, Eugene and Ellamae Elder began to feel a new stirring in their lives, which led them to the city of East London in South Africa. There they served as missionaries during tumultuous years of political upheaval that led to the ascension of Nelson Mandela into political power in the post-apartheid era. Ellamae moved from "stranger in a foreign land" to neighbor, friend, mentor, sister and adopted parent. As a talented and experienced seamstress, she equipped impoverished women with an income-producing skill while using every opportunity to share the gospel message.

Strange sounding names like "Chalumna", "Keiskammahoek", and "Dongwe" will take on new meaning as you read of the moving and working of the Holy Spirit. In this book, the heart and life of an ordinary missionary is laid open. Here you will find the struggles, fears, hopes, and victories of ordinary people serving an extraordinary God.

Read this book and be inspired and challenged to grow and perhaps, GO yourself. This book will remind you that God is on His throne, and history is running right on time. He has a plan for your life. May God use *In His Shelter* to help you on your way.

--DR. GORDON FORT, Senior Ambassador to the President, International Mission Board of the Southern Baptist Convention

When most people are planning for retirement, Eugene and Ellamae Elder were considering what the Lord might have for their future. Leaving behind grown children, grandchildren, and the comfort of the known, the Elders followed God's call to South Africa. *In His Shelter* is a record of God's faithfulness when we say "yes." Elder is transparent as she recounts both struggles and victories as they shared Jesus.

--CANDACE MCINTOSH, Executive Director of Alabama Baptist Women's Missionary Union

Through affliction, war, tragedy, language barriers and celebrations, God is faithful. You will be pulled through a winding road of civil unrest, internal turmoil, and miracles that can only be explained by a Divine power. This is a gripping memoir of a pastor and his wife who were "aged out" of becoming missionaries and how God used them in South Africa amidst civil unrest. Through sewing classes, tracts, and English lessons, Ellamae was able to spread the Gospel while also giving us an inside look at the realities of mental health struggles in our missionaries. But she maneuvered through it all by clinging to restoration, hope, and rest that only comes through a relationship with Jesus Christ. While Christ is enough, we discover how invaluable the gift of friendships and spiritual family are. Community is vital, not optional.

--CRYSTAL MARQUIS, Physician Assistant at Pinon Family Practice, Church Planting Wife

The Word became flesh is God's staggering plan to rescue a broken world. His Son Jesus will empty himself and give his life away on a Roman cross. He calls his disciples and followers to venture out with him in trust and reckless faith. The Elders' reflections and journey into the troubled fields of apartheid South Africa and post-election days provide challenge and insight into what it means to follow Jesus. Every mission story is unique, bold, and a challenge to move out from our safe lives of settledness, routine, and comfort. This read will not disappoint.

--DR. DAVID CRUTCHLEY, Dean, School of Biblical and Theological Studies, Carson- Newman University

Having become an octogenarian after fourteen years into retirement, I entered into what many would identify as the final season of life. I was badgered by the question of how to use the years God has given me to contribute to His kingdom. As Gene and Ellamae Elder faced this issue, it resulted in a decision to go back to the mission field. As a gifted storyteller, Ellamae's stories of their time in southern Africa will amaze and inspire the reader. The villages and people will come alive as she navigates cross-cultural experiences. They will also thrill one's heart at how God used the wisdom and maturity of a gray-haired witness to gain respect and change lives through her faithful witness, Bible studies, and discipling local believers. The Elders' willingness to give these advanced years to the Lord and boldness to leave the normal comforts most live for in retirement, and endure austere living conditions on the mission field will challenge those who read their testimony to greater devotion and faithfulness whatever the season of life.

--JERRY RANKIN, President Emeritus, International Mission Board

One Sunday morning, my pastor, Gene Elder, announced to his congregation that he and his wife, Ellamae, had decided to leave his congregation in Aztec, New Mexico, and travel to South Africa as foreign missionaries. In answering God's call, they were leaving behind their home, grown children, grandchildren, and a church family who loved them, to embark on a journey of service, sacrifice, and love in order to bring the light of Jesus into a lost and dark place of turmoil.

In her book *In His Shelter*, Ellamae recounts the adventures, joys, sorrows, fears, and miracles that she experienced in South Africa. In trial after trial, she found her shelter in the "shadow of His wings" and her strength in the promises of God's Word. Hers is an amazing story of courage and perseverance while she used her gifts as teacher, musician, and seamstress to bring the gospel of Christ to a lost generation. Reading her story will challenge you to answer God's call whenever it comes and trust Him to lead you.

--CAROLYN COX, Colleague and former Educator of twenty-five years